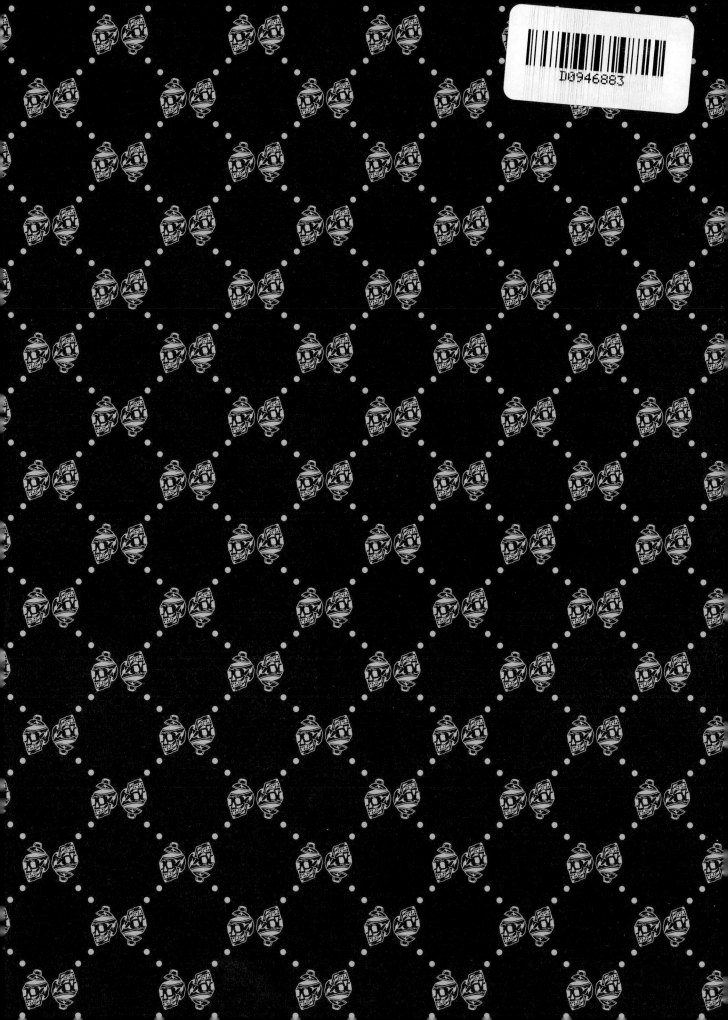

BLACK AXE MANGAL

BLACK AXE MANGAL

LEE TIERNAN

FOREWORD
FERGUS HENDERSON

It is a fact for every one of us that other people's perception of us is quite different to our own. And then, the more you are written about and photographed, the more this other character takes hold in the public consciousness. In my case I watch the progress of the public Fergus Henderson with interest, torn between dismay at the portrayals of a Tweedledee, Pooh Bear–like demeanour which I only vaguely recognize as me, and secret delight that my interior passions remain thrillingly my own. I am like Clark Kent, but my glasses stay on (gathering steam) and my superpower is a tireless capacity for too much tequila and 5 a.m. dancing. I find Black Axe Mangal to be an excellent starting point for such a transformation.

I have often said that a chef should make like a whale, keeping their hungry mouth wide open for the plankton of ideas. That sifting mechanism is vital – tune in to the vibrations around you! Go out late in strange cities; if you choose your companions well then inspiration is just as likely to strike in the 5 a.m. tequila haze as it is when chained to the oven, and no one knows this better than Lee.

St. JOHN has been part of his plankton – a nutritious contribution to his might – but his diet has been varied and he has always been totally, admirably and wonderfully himself. Where St. JOHN plays no music, Black Axe Mangal resounds with it. Where St. JOHN's tablecloths and walls are white, Black Axe is loudly blousy with plastic flowers. There is something of the religious cult about it, recruiting by sensory overload, hot and loud, heady and delicious. Its followers are fervent.

Lee's intent and singularity was always evident. Some time ago we were in New York to cook and we ate too (ah, and bounteously!), but the excellent wine I ordered did not interest Lee. He was focused on the dry martinis drunk in the Four Seasons. Above us in the bar hung, as always, that sculpture composed of a forest of menacing spikes, pointing downwards, threatening our impalement at any moment. Martinis are focussing at the best of times, but we found that proximity to imminent death added a piquancy, a new dimension to a dry martini. Lee was so taken by it that he had the glass tattooed on his leg.

On another occasion, in Nashville, a taste of mortality was provided by a bucking bronco, which Lee rode wildly, intensely and very momentarily (he was followed by two blond-haired twins who rode it together, spectacularly, but suffered an even shorter fate). This adventure preceded a near-stabbing later that night from which we were saved by our host Pat Martin, owner of a fantastic barbecue restaurant where we had lunched copiously on every type of animal, wearer of American football shirts which require no padding on his huge frame, and blessed with such internal force that he was able to project his stream of piss clear over a parked car.

The most extraordinary thing about Lee has always been his determination; he has always known exactly what he wanted. He has the most remarkable clarity and sense of purpose and, with his wife Kate, their private passions are joyfully expressed in their restaurant. Lee is a master of the crispy pig skin, a squid-ink dark magician. There is a cosmic riot of glitter, the taming of amorphous tofu and the heady hit of numbing spice. Lee has borrowed my bone marrow, my cod's roe, my pig's blood, but they are not what shape him. We are part of a fraternity but he has never sacrificed a sense of ambitious certainty and shame-less self. I am proud to be a mother hen, nurturing my chicks and sending them out into the world to see what form they take. Lee has become a hard rock eagle – but that is exactly the bird that he has always been.

St. JOHN
DOES NOT ACCEPT
ANY RESPONSIBILITY
FOR PERSONAL
BELONGINGS

INTRODUCTION

PHIPPS BRIDGE

Before the age of twenty five, I had zero interest in becoming a cook, even less interest in working in a restaurant, and very limited experience of eating out. When I asked my mum about what my eating habits were as a child, she said she'd taken me to see a doctor because of my reluctance to eat. Apparently, every food was met with protest, which for the most part led to point-blank refusal. A little cheese, sometimes bread and lots of milk is all I'd happily consume. My mum remembers one particular low when her frustration got the better of her after three previous dinner attempts and several tantrums, and she dumped a bowl of cold Spaghetti Hoops on my head. I hid a multitude of meals I didn't like under a loose floorboard in the back room, my unwitting parents delighted to think I'd started actually finishing my food. Unfortunately, Dad did eventually discover my decayed stash years later when we were replacing the gas pipes. My other foray into concealment was a bowl of Rice Krispies under a mat, which my poor mum thought was a maggot infestation when she stood on it. Needless to say, my attitude towards food changed slowly as I grew older... To the point that I'm now writing a cookbook, for fuck's sake.

I'm from a large, close, Irish Catholic family, and I decided I wanted to believe in God when I was about five years old, not just play along anymore. I prayed for two things: one, that my parents wouldn't make any brothers and sisters to keep me company, and two, that they would stay together forever. I've long since turned my back on religion, but for the time I had God's ear, he seemed to listen, and to this day I am still an only child, and my parents have been married for forty years. My mum is an excellent cook, as were both my nans, so in turn, all my aunties are skilled in the kitchen. We would congregate at my nan and grandad's house on Glentanner Way, Tooting, South London, most weekends. It's staggering to think my nan fed so many of our hungry mouths from such a tiny kitchen; everything was made from scratch, with the smell of gravy lingering and ever-present condensation on the windows from boiling cabbage and gammon. I became obsessed with roast potatoes, and to this day I suffer genuine panic if there is even the slightest possibility that I can't eat my fill of spuds at a family gathering.

I grew up on the Phipps Bridge Estate in the London Borough of Merton. (Big up Phipps Massive.) When I looked up Phipps Bridge on Wikipedia, it painted an ignorant, biased, bleak picture of the place I was raised and proud to be from – so fuck you, Wikipedia. Like any housing estate, Phipps Bridge might not have been idyllic and has had its fair share of ups and downs, but there was always a strong sense of community and loyalty towards each other, and I still experience feelings of homesickness to this day. My parents were dedicated members of that community; mum worked at the local youth centre day and night, while my dad volunteered at the same place and was involved in local projects run by her. He also became a Labour councillor for a spell, while at the same time holding down a full-time job as an electrician.

The week before I started high school, my mum showed me how to use the washing machine, tumble dryer and iron, making me responsible for keeping my school uniform clean and pressed, which at the time felt like unjustifiable persecution, but in hindsight put me on the path of independence. I even started to feed myself from time to time, too. I'd cook boil-in-the-bag cod in butter, pour it on top of pasta and cover it in a thick layer of chilli flakes, and if I felt keen, I would finesse the dish with a few slices of raw red pepper. I should have recognized the signs of creative genius then, but I wouldn't say that's where my aspirations of being a chef began. In truth, I liked a microwave meal best. Cooking, like the washing and ironing, was something that had to happen every now and again, and I was marginally more enthusiastic about cooking. I mean, how enthusiastic can anyone ever get about washing and ironing? Most kids are like that – most adults are like that. There are moments when I still have that attitude. I'm too lazy to make toast sometimes, especially if the bread needs to be sliced, and I prefer Nescafé because I don't have to wait for the coffee to dribble through a filter. I'm into instant gratification. I can't suck a lollipop, I have to crunch it almost immediately. I often say I always choose the path of least resistance, however, it's also true that I'm hyper-aware of the fact that if there's a way of over-complicating something, especially in the kitchen, then I will. But I've made my peace with being a hypocrite.

Curry was the first thing I got genuinely excited about eating. We only had dinner out on special occasions; most anniversaries or birthdays, me, my mum and dad would get dressed up and take a short drive to a little Indian restaurant called Samrat in Tooting. It was quality time I shared with my parents and there was a real sense of occasion. We rarely wavered in our ritual: always onion bhajis, and at least ten poppadoms. Mum would order dhansak, okra and spinach, and Dad would have vindaloo and Bombay potatoes. I began with korma and branched out to madras over the years we ate there as a family, and I've never lost my weakness for mango kulfi. We'd sit in the same booth every visit, Mum and I squeezing in next to the wall, Dad sitting opposite. I have a keen sense of smell, and my memories are often triggered by it. I remember the stab of anticipation I'd get from the car to the restaurant; the anticipation of a meal I couldn't wait to eat, and also because I knew I would get to smell *that* smell: the sweet and sour combination of onions cooking in spices, chillies, breads, and those aggressive sizzle platters. The aromas were intoxicating, and the food was exotic and supremely tasty. The staff made us feel like we were the most important people in the room. The service was effortless and warm – they helped us on with our coats, gave my mum a red rose on the way out, and handed me a couple of extra After Eight chocolates. I'd have given out the roses at BAM too, if our budget could have stretched to it. The Samrat of my youth never changed.

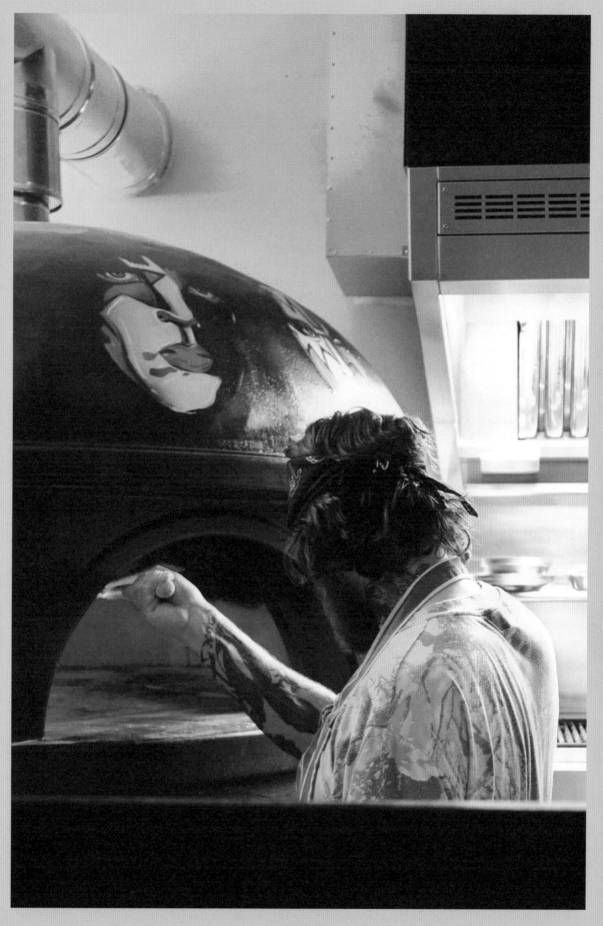

When I left school (which I hated) I started working at Ede's Removals – the money was good, and I liked the camaraderie. I was still living with my mum and dad, which I would've happily continued to do indefinitely. Then one night, I got drunk at a neighbour's house, and they told me about their time in Thailand, and suggested I should explore the world a bit, see something new. The idea stuck, and when I'd saved enough money, I bought a one-way ticket to Bangkok. Three days after arriving in the city, I was in a travel agent trying to get a flight back to the UK. It was so fucking hectic. I suffered a huge bout of culture shock, and I was already homesick. I managed to talk myself out of leaving, largely because I didn't want to deal with the shame of returning home so soon, although it did cross my mind that I could fly back and live in a different part of England for a while and not tell anyone. But instead, I headed north to Ayutthaya, where things were more mellow. I saw an elephant when the bus pulled into the station, I wandered round a temple for all of an hour, then spent the next couple of days and nights propping up a local bar. I couldn't believe how much Thai people love Premiership football. I watched Arsenal versus Manchester United that first night; Thierry Henry scored an unstoppable wonder volley, and suddenly I didn't feel so homesick. I got chatting to a group of people after the match, and we ended up sticking together for the best part of a year. I ate and drank my way around Asia for a while after, and had a brief stint in Sydney, Australia, but then returned to Thailand to run a bar for while. Well, I say 'run' a bar, really, I smoked fags, drank beer and played Scrabble for a living (personal best score 516).

Eventually it felt time to move on, so I went to the US Virgin Island of St John, of all places, with the promise of some well paid work and a place to stay. Everyone was super cool, and the island is a true paradise, but as it turned out, there wasn't much work to be had. I did a bit of labouring for cash, but that was about the extent of it. I got to know the chefs at a bar and restaurant that my friend worked in, and they would feed me lunch through the back window. One day, a chef didn't show up for his shift, and knowing I needed the cash, they asked me to step in for the night. I obviously decided to keep my aforementioned boil-in-the-bag-style cooking prowess to myself, and being desperate for the money, jumped straight in. I managed to get through the night, and did an okay job, I think... This all sounds very by proxy, and it really was – if I'd have gotten a job on a building site, I might well be a builder now. I didn't feel under any pressure because it was just for one night, and a bit of fun. I worked the next night, and then the absent chef returned to work. By then, though, I was hooked – the kitchen had the same camaraderie, drinking culture and filthy language as the removals company, except it was better, because I got to play with knives and fire – Anthony Bourdain used to call it 'crew mentality'. The appreciation for the craft of actual cooking, of course, came later.

A couple of weeks after that, I got word from my dad that my nan was dying, so I returned home to say goodbye. By that point, I'd maxed out my credit card, and my parents had been depositing money into my account for a month, so they had to send me the cash for a return flight to England. After the funeral, I was at home living with Mum and Dad again, back working at the same removals company. It was like I'd never been away at all, and that depressed me, so when I saw an ad in the local paper for a catering NVQ at Carshalton College, I decided to apply. I always struggled at school but found the practical element of cooking rewarding, and I was surprised to find I was actually pretty good at it. The written element of the course I found impossible, and I relied on a couple of kind classmates to help me out so I wouldn't fail. I got a job at a local pub to pay my way, in a quasi commis chef role. It was pretty shit food, but working there taught me what I didn't want to cook, and what I needed to achieve if I was going to take cooking seriously. To complete the qualification at the end of the course, all the students had to do a two-week placement in a restaurant. I had little knowledge of the London dining scene at this point, but knew 100% I didn't want to be stuck in the pub I was working in for those two weeks. I'd been reading *A Cook's Tour* by Anthony Bourdain and in the chapter 'Fire Over London', he talked about Fergus Henderson and St. JOHN restaurant. I was attracted to the dialogue between Anthony and Fergus. Fergus seemed interesting and not in the least bit intimidating. Someone I could work for. I reasoned that St. JOHN would be a good restaurant to do my two-week placement in, so I gave them a call…

THE ST. JOHN YEARS

Head Chef Edwin Lewis picked up the phone at St. JOHN, and I arranged to go in for a chat about the possibility of a two-week stage at the restaurant. I'd been involved in a stupid drunken brawl the night before I was due to meet Ed and I must have looked like absolute shit. I almost didn't go because I thought they would take one look at me with cuts and bruises and say, 'Thanks, but no thanks.' Ed was very welcoming, though, and was polite enough not to mention the state of my face. We agreed I would do my stage there, and, two weeks later, I turned up at St. JOHN restaurant for my first shift.

After helping get the deliveries away and familiarizing myself with the refrigerator, the first task I was given was to bone out an entire sirloin. Jesus fucking Christ. It must have been painful to watch, but Ed was infinitely patient and guided me through it. Next job, bone and roll pigs' heads for Bath chaps, stick them in the brine bucket and record the entry on the brine table – what an introduction to cooking. I went home feeling like I would learn a lot over the next two weeks, and decided instantly that my aim was to work at St. JOHN in the future. The chefs were all so cool, too; no shouting, but lots of laughter and respect for each other.

A few days into my stage, one of the chefs de partie handed in his notice. Ed called me down to the bar and asked if I'd like a beer. I thought he was going to say I couldn't see out my stage – I had just thrown away all the skin I'd removed from the Middle White pork assuming it was waste, which of course at St. JOHN, it wasn't. 'What are you doing after you finish your stage?' he asked. 'Looking for a job,' I said, to which he replied, 'What would you say if I offered you a job here?' To which I replied 'I would say yes...' Later that day, I met Fergus.

It took me a couple of days to adjust to the situation. It's embarrassing to admit, but at this point in time, I hadn't even eaten at St. JOHN, and was only recently aware of its calibre. A fact I hadn't mentioned to anyone because no one asked, but I knew it was a pretty unusual situation. As a result, that's the first question I ask anyone applying for a job: 'You eaten here?'

I've spent many hours staring at my screen trying to come up with a phrase or a word that describes my first meal at St. JOHN without sounding clichéd or corny. And I've come to the conclusion that I actually can't. I was just blown away. Champagne, Boiled Egg and Celery Salt, Bone Marrow and Parsley Salad, Ox Heart and Pickled Walnut, Tripe, Cured Beef, Braised Hare (thickened with blood) and Swede, Welsh Rarebit, Lemon Sorbet and Russian Vodka, Baked Chocolate Mousse – all washed down with Fernet-Branca. So yes, blown away, elated and intimidated by my lack of knowledge and experience, but determined to work my arse off for these people. After that meal, everything changed. I fully committed to my new job and had the privilege of working at St. JOHN for a little over a decade, meeting my wife (and business partner) Kate there, and leaving as Head Chef of St. JOHN Bread and Wine in 2013. The opportunities and experiences afforded me during my time working for Trevor (St. JOHN's co-founder) and Fergus are incomparable, and I hold dear the memories forged over all those years, and our friendship that remains to this day.

WHEN KATE MET LEE, AS TOLD BY KATE TIERNAN

I was introduced to Lee in 2005 at my first St. JOHN Christmas party, and he was very chatty. I remember clearly two things he said to me that night: one, that he loved St. JOHN, and that Fergus Henderson was the greatest chef he knew and two, that he would never leave the company. I recall feeling surprised by his enthusiasm and commitment to his job – he genuinely loved it in a way that most people don't feel about work. I would never have guessed that night, or in fact for many after, that within two years we'd be madly in love and married.

I've worked in some form of restaurant since I was 16; I tried other stuff, but always returned to hospitality. First off, I liked the pace, the theatre of it all, and to be honest, the cash. In the olden days, cash tips were the thing you waitressed for, that and the free food and booze – both are highly addictive. I was once employed at a place called Wild Jack Henry's. We'd do three sittings serving platters of meat and chips, and before dessert the entertainment started, which was two men dressed as cowboys pretending to have a gun fight in the middle of the restaurant. As I was clearing tables, a parade of dancing girls would mount them and do their routine before the diners headed upstairs to learn how to line dance. The food was undeniably terrible, but it was wildly fun because they really knew how to show people a good time. Years later, working for St. JOHN was a stark contrast. Don't get me wrong – people were, and still are, having a good time, but it's the food they are there for. Their idea of entertainment is watching the busy chefs in the kitchen, and the star performers are dishes on the menu. It is a place to learn about food and true hospitality, where there are no frills and there is no nonsense. The best thing about working (and dining) at St. JOHN is the union between guest, server and chef: all parties are equal in terms of knowledge and enjoyment. Both restaurants serve as bench marks for me when I think about how I want our guests to feel when they dine at BAM.

THE KEBAB SHOP IDEA

Bread, specifically flatbread, was the catalyst for Black Axe Mangal, even though at the time, I didn't realize it. The obsession began while I was head chef at St. JOHN Bread and Wine, and Kate and I were a million miles from entertaining the concept of leaving to open a place of our own. I had been frequenting Turkish mangals in London as often as I could for years, with their fresh bread being one of the major draws. As a result, I had started testing bread recipes at home whenever I had the time; again and again, it failed to meet the flavour and texture I had in my head. I knew what I wanted to achieve, but didn't have much of an idea of how to get there, and little actual understanding of the intricacies of how bread behaves. With that running in parallel, so it was that in Copen-hagen on 3 July 2012, the seed of what would come to be known as BAM was planted.

I had gone along to that year's MAD symposium (an annual two-day industry event founded by René Redzepi to discuss the future of food and our industry), and the day after the closing party, I was hungover like never before after a big night out at the now-closed Sam's Bar, and in desperate need of something greasy to eat. I walked into the first kebab shop I happened to be passing and ordered a shish. While waiting for the kebab I reflected on the symposium; I listened to many fascinating talks and met some incredible people over the weekend. One talk in particular resonated with me. I felt deeply moved and utterly inspired by Anthony Myint and Danny Bowien's presentation 'The Audacity of Hope... and Szechuan Peppercorns'. The kebab arrived, and the first bite dragged me back from the brink of oblivion. That kebab satisfied my soul on a level like nothing I had ever eaten before. Thoughts of Danny and Anthony's talk and the pleasure I was experiencing from eating the kebab synthesized into one crystal-clear vision: 'This is what I want to cook, this is what I'm am going to cook.' My mental culinary trajectory started moving in a totally different direction.

I wrote down a list of dishes and ideas for the restaurant on the plane home. A few days later, I introduced the idea to Kate of opening a kebab shop, which she admittedly thought was bonkers at first. I was confident it would work, and I'd been attracted to open fire cooking for a while. I just had to get the bread right... As I said, it had become an obsession, and I had severely underestimated how difficult it was to make a decent flatbread. I must have tried close to a hundred recipes – some were okay, most were shite, and none came close to the quality I wanted to accomplish (I eventually managed to perfect a recipe with help from Chad Robertson of Tartine Bakery, see page 56). So after my initial excitement, I held on to my ideas, but didn't talk much about my concept. I was very happy working at St. JOHN Bread and Wine, and shit scared of striking out on my own.

THE ROAD TO COPENHAGEN, AS TOLD BY KATE TIERNAN

Lee first told me he wanted to open a kebab shop while we were both working at Bread and Wine. He was inspired by a trip to MAD in Copenhagen, and my reaction was less than impressed. I remember thinking 'that was money well spent, so glad you went to this event full of internationally acclaimed chefs to return with this lofty aspiration'. It took a long time for me to come around to the idea. But there is a timing alchemy to life, and shortly after he had his kebab epiphany, Lee's grandfather died and left him some money, and my brother Andrew offered to give us some money to do our own thing, too. The time felt ripe, so we left our jobs and decided to do something different for a while.

Whilst we looked for a site in East London, Lee travelled with the aim of learning what he could from whoever was willing to teach him. The idea was pretty pure – find a small, cheap site, make great food and have fun doing it. We enlisted the help of

an artist friend, Charlie Woolley, who sent us cool images to choose from for our logo, and helped reason through Lee's rantings to find a name for the enterprise. We went to Istanbul with Charlie and feasted together, sitting up late talking, drinking and fantasizing about what the restaurant would be like. In the end it didn't work out with Charlie, but his enthusiasm at the beginning was very important. The invite came from the lads in Copenhagen to run a pop-up for the summer in 2014, and we found no reason to say no as neither of us were working. Actually, I would have said no if I had ever been to Bakken, but Lee navigated the situation well. He's a good salesperson by nature, optimistic and great at leaving out important stuff that might put you off something. I had briefly lived in Copenhagen before, so felt confident we would have a good time. I found us an Airbnb, Lee filled our car with everything he felt he needed (this included a smoker, numerous pots and pans and a jar of kefir) and we set off. For the first week our kids weren't with us, which was a good thing, as it wasn't quite what I had expected...

BAKKEN SPECIAL, AS TOLD BY LARS ERIKSEN, VICE DENMARK

None of it really made any sense on paper, but that was the beauty of Black Axe Mangal at Bakken. For six weeks during the summer of 2014, Lee and Kate took over the backyard of a grimy, graffiti-smeared Copenhagen night club and cooked kebabs in a ramshackle shed where the bartenders normally dispensed six packs of Carlsberg and liquorice-spiked shots. It was a bonkers fusion of booze, ravers, chilli oil and smoked lamb shoulder.

Lee and I started to carve out the idea when we met in London a few months previously. The premise for this was going to be primal – kebabs and beer – but it needed to be the right venue. Lee had already worked with our mutual friends in Copenhagen who ran the café Dyrehaven in Vesterbro and Bakken in the Meatpacking district. Located in an old white-tiled butcher's shop, Bakken has the aesthetic delicacy of a hardcore metal mosh pit, and somehow it was the perfect match: Lee wanted to test his idea of grilling flatbreads and Bakken wanted to use their backyard for more than serving the occasional cheese on toast to souped-up revellers in the early hours of the evening.

When Kate arrived at Bakken for the first time, after the morning cleaners had scraped down the debris, she noted the distinct smell of booze and bleach; Lee seemed to thrive on that smell. They set up shop in the backyard and installed the beaten-up smoker they had dragged across Europe in the car from London. Everything in the run-up to the launch was a mad scramble. Sorting our flyers, getting the barbecue working and convincing the local suppliers that yes, we did want them to drop off boxes of ox hearts to a night club.

On the opening Friday in July, none of us had a clue as to whether we would end up serving just the two bouncers on the door. The idea was to give away a bunch of free kebabs on the first night, just to build some initial momentum and maybe draw in a few extra people, but instead there was bedlam. Before we even opened the doors to the club, a queue of about 200 people was snaking its way through the Meatpacking district.

Helping Lee out on the grill on the first night was Jesper, one of the Bakken owners, and me. In the end, one of the bouncers had to step in to help cook flatbreads on a camping stove in the corner of the shed. We were fucked, plain and simple, covered in flour and sweat. It was one of the greatest Friday nights of my life.

Lee, on the other hand, looked like he was ready to hide behind the kegs in the walk-in refrigerator. He had given away hundreds of kebabs for free, there was no more fermented potato bread, no more pickled red cabbage and no more smoked lamb shoulder. As we turned away the last people who had queued for an hour, Lee told Jesper: 'That's it. I'm done. I'm never doing this again!' All Lee really wanted to do, he said before the opening, was to take every drug known to mankind and sink into oblivion, but as the rest of us were getting smashed in the club after service, he only drank bottles of fizzy water (in Danish, *danskvand*).Much to our annoyance, and much to the success of this endeavour, Lee stayed sober the whole time he was at Bakken: 'I have to stick to danskvand these six weeks if I want to get through this'.

We got through it alright, high on danskvand, ear-bleedingly loud Pantera and 'Deepthroater' kebabs with grilled ox hearts. Things were never quite as chaotic as that first night again, but the hungry punters kept coming. Kate and Lee sold out every night, Action Bronson came to eat, and Black Axe became an integral part of Bakken that summer. All credit for this high-jinks collaboration should go to the people behind Bakken – Jesper and his co-owners Nikolaj and Jens Ole – but it seemed like everybody else involved with the club got stuck in. From Michael, Bakken's tireless PR hypeman, to bartenders cleaning up pans while serving shots and the club manager, who became pretty proficient at chopping onions.

Chef friends came and helped Lee on the grill, including Tom Adams from the now-closed Pitt Cue in London and Tom Halpin, a former sous-chef at Noma. One morning during prep, Halpin chopped off the tip of his finger while trimming ox hearts. He was rushed to hospital and Lee called in assistance from Ian Moore, a former promoter at Bakken who was another regular fixture in the woodshed kitchen. 'Tom called from the hospital to find out if we still had the tip so the doctors could stitch it back on,' remembers Ian, 'but Lee had flicked the rest of it off the knife and into the bin. The rest of the finger was gone.' Two hours later, Halpin came back from hospital and finished the rest of the evening service with his hand wrapped up in gauze and raised in the air,

while swinging tongs in the other. At this point, such madness seemed like par for the course.

The summer ended with another blowout; more free kebabs and food royalty in the crowd, which packed out Bakken on the final night of BAM's residency. It was a fitting sign-off, but the magic of that summer was watching the day-to-day evolution of Black Axe, observing the bizarre blend of people trying to run one of Copenhagen's most feral night spots with a chef winning people over to his freewheeling take on kebabs.

At times it looked like torture behind that grill, or when Kate and Lee spent the weekdays alone in the club, smoking lamb shoulders and prepping for the weekend. Lee's face always looked like it was etched with equal amounts of passion and pain. 'I don't want to sound like I'm whinging, but I'm not the best person to run a restaurant,' Lee told me. 'It's the pressure. It's like sitting at home watching TV and all of a sudden your wife opens the door and goes, "right, get hard! I want to fuck you!" That's my analogy of running a restaurant. I constantly have to get it up. Get it hard.'

For six weeks during the summer of 2014, Lee got it hard every night. I love Black Axe Mangal on the Highbury and Islington roundabout. It's the perfect manifestation of Kate and Lee's ideas and their middle-finger salute to conventions, but to some of us, Black Axe Mangal will always belong in Copenhagen. Part of it will always belong in the backyard of Bakken.

THE BIG BAM THEORY

Without the relentless and infinite support and help of our parents, family, friends and staff, Black Axe Mangal would never have opened its doors.

Opening BAM was a terrifying experience. It's sounds like a cliché, but it really was akin to a rollercoaster. All the time I was on the ride I was feeling 'I should be enjoying this'; 'revel in this experience'; 'this is your time!', but all the while I was just shitting my pants desperate for the ride to end... even writing this now, I'm feeling that stab of stress and revisiting feelings I'm reluctant to confront. The intimidation I felt opening a restaurant dissolved my confidence and stifled any creative flow I had possessed in the build-up to the first service. If all I had to contribute to the opening was to get a menu ready for night one, I would have still struggled and have happily procrastinated indefinitely. I'd made the decision to abstain from drinking alcohol while we were in the process of opening BAM, as I did for the pop-up in Copenhagen. I've used alcohol as a coping mechanism for as long as I can remember, but as I've grown older, when I've felt a stressful situation looming large, I've found that total abstinence decreases my chances of meltdown and gives me a better ability

to gain clarity and centre myself. Being shitfaced with the pressure affecting me the way it did would have only led to oblivion.

The fact that Kate and I were making decisions about every aspect of the build, fit-out, equipment, staff and everything else that goes with opening a restaurant just added to the pressure I was feeling. Having this experience was a privilege I'd fantasized about, and now I just wanted to bury my head under my pillow and for someone to tell me the monsters weren't real and everything was going to be okay. All our friends and family rallied around, but ultimately the person who held it all together was Kate. On top of being pregnant with our third child, she absorbed so much of my anxiety in the build-up I'm surprised she didn't lose it herself. Fast forward to opening night with a full dining room 2 minutes after opening our doors, and with a line of customers down the road... I'd have happily locked the door to that restaurant and walked away never to return.

The opening night menu was short, cheap and a touch on the desperate side. Portions were generous and the execution could have been better. I felt like I had to deliver food that people wanted to eat, so that was how I designed the menu. This frustrated me and I felt like I was compromising. All this stress to compromise on the menu? Kate sensed my reservations and said something that defined our approach at BAM to this day. 'Does it have to be Turkish? Why don't you cook things you love to eat and cook rather than trying to make all this other stuff? We can do what we want here, we aren't cooking for anyone but us, we are in control and we can change whatever, whenever we want.'

I'm pretty confident Kate had said this to me before, I just hadn't heard her, because I was convinced that my idea was the best. The next day I brought my stash of Mission Chinese spice into work, made an XO sauce and bought some century eggs ready for the second evening's menu. I had more confidence in the food that night, and felt a touch lighter, even allowing myself a sliver of excitement at the prospect of cooking and serving this menu. That night Fay Maschler, London's longest standing food critic, came (and waited patiently like everyone else) to dine at Black Axe Mangal with her dear husband Reg, which destroyed any fleeting excitement I might have been feeling, even though the resulting review more than made up for it.

So when did things start to get better? The more services we got under our belts, the more I started to regain the confidence to try new things and use bolder flavours and ideas. Instead of trying to cater for the 90 per cent of diners, we focused on the 10 per cent. Of that 10 per cent, about 7 per cent of the people coming through our doors really got what we were doing. We had a growing number of regulars, which made the difference some nights when the restaurant was full of people asking to turn the music down or complaining about how hot the food was, or how numbing the Mission Spice is. Our restaurant is not for these people and just to make it abundantly clear... again... if you don't like cramped, loud restaurants that serve spicy food without prioritizing a particular cuisine, please do not come to BAM. These gripes and

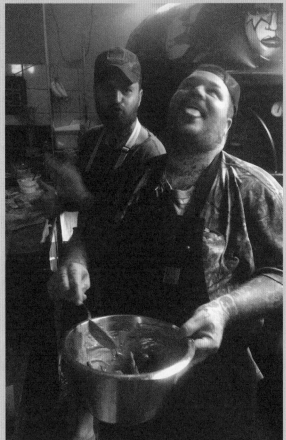

grumbles did help us hone our attitude, however, playing an important part in the make up of Black Axe Mangal today.

The first shift I missed at Black Axe was the night before our son Elvis was born, and guess what? The restaurant survived the night, customers were happy, and no one died. I started to enjoy BAM more when I started to care about it in a different way and reached more of a balance. By stepping back every now and again, I could see more of what we had achieved and our future potential. It had *almost* become fun at this point. We have always been blessed with a dedicated, caring body of staff without which (like every other restaurant in the world) we simply couldn't function. In the end, we managed to create the restaurant we had set out to: somewhere fun and creative, that doesn't take itself too seriously, and with genre-fluid cuisine that reflects the diversity of London and its people. But why didn't anyone tell me how ridiculous I look in a fucking bandana?

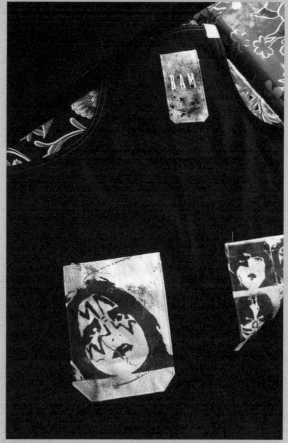

GRILLING
SMOKING
BREAD

As I grew as a cook, I explored other chefs' work, but felt frustrated when the recipe called for equipment that was completely unrealistic in a domestic kitchen. When I started to cook in a professional capacity, I began to understand and accept that if you wanted to achieve the same results as an amazing chef with access to the best equipment, then the only way to exactly replicate it was with the same equipment. I suppose that's why I've never been attracted to the idea of writing a 'this is what we do in the restaurant but you'll never be able to achieve it at home' cookbook, as much as I've never been attracted to writing something generic. I want us to have fun with this book together. I've tried where possible to suggest alternatives to ingredients and equipment without diluting what we produce at **BAM**.

When it comes to these techniques, I can't give you guarantees, because they require a little bit of intuition, and a decent amount of practice; that is the biggest anxiety about writing a cookbook that's based around smoking, grilling and bread making. But I think you would be right to expect detailed methods and some reassurance. I know I did when I first started cooking and relied on chefs like Jamie Oliver (someone who deserves more credit than he is given for changing the **UK**'s attitude towards cooking) to provide me with the answers to my questions, not cost me any more money in ingredients than I'd already spent, and most importantly, give me precise information that I could interpret, which would develop a confidence in achieving a good result from a recipe I wanted to try out.

The techniques you will read about here have accompanying step-by-step pictures, all of which were taken in my home kitchen and back garden, with my most basic equipment. The one thing that all of these techniques have in common is that decent preparation, and patience, will make all the difference. Making the effort to organize your time and equipment will take the majority of the stress out of cooking in general. This is advice coming from a man who has to make a conscious decision to be organized, someone who knows that the effort it takes to organize one's self can feel like a hassle, but ultimately saves time and stress in the long run. I understand that this is a healthier attitude towards cooking, having worked in an environment that punishes you if you cut a corner or forget a key element through disorganization – something I've experienced more times than I like to admit. In possession of this valuable knowledge gained over many years in the kitchen, I still choose to ignore it at times. Luckily, I am supported daily by people who excel at being organized, but not everyone has that luxury, so it's down to you which path you follow and how much stress you put yourself under. Hopefully with this guidance I can show you what to look for.

The grill at **BAM** is far too big. It's a fire-brick lined, stainless steel-coated brute fuelled by a combination of long-burning compressed charcoal and lump wood charcoal. The long burners provide the heat, and the charcoal the flavour. The grills are heavy cast iron for maximum heat retention. We use half the grill for grilling and the other half for resting meats and keeping plates warm. But no matter what size grill I'm cooking on, I mostly use the off-set method, in which you create a spectrum of high to low heat across a grill by heaping all the coals to one side. This gives you two extremes of hot and cool, and of course everything in between. I've written all the grilling recipes with this heat range in mind. You gain that much more control when you have a hot zone and a cooler zone – it gives you options. We use the highest heat to colour meats and grill cuts like heart and liver that benefit from a short hard cook. The medium heat is used to char vegetables, and the low section is for rendering and crisping fat on our impossibly fatty pork chops from **Farmer Tom's** pigs. Larger meat skewers are best cooked just shy of the coolest section, giving them colour over a longer period of time.

What attracts me to grilling is the instantaneousness (wow I can't believe that is a word) of it – no waiting for pans to get hot or water to boil. I love the smell that comes off a grill too, it's primal and insanely appetizing. The whole visual aspect to grilling with the flare ups and the sound of the meat sizzling and charcoal spitting makes it a multi-sensory experience. You can use all these indicators to understand where the grill is at and how the heat behaves. If you place a chop on the grill and it doesn't make a satis-fying kkkiiiiisssssssshhhhhhcccccc, then the grill or that particular part of the grill isn't hot enough. If you're getting mad flare up, then you are grilling your meat over too high a heat. Think of it this way... when a pan of water hits the boil on a gas stove, you can reduce to a simmer by turning the heat down. Apply this idea to the grill by utilizing the hotter and cooler zones to provide varied levels of heat.

GRILL ZONES

I always set up my grill so that the hottest zone is on the left and coolest on the right, but this is a habit, not a rule. The zones will depend on the size of your grill or barbecue. If you have a tiny barbecue, bear in mind that your zoning will be limited.

ZONE 1

This is the hottest zone. At **BAM** this side of the grill may as well be tapped into the earth's core. Use this extreme heat to char herbs and any meat that calls for quick, intense cooking, such as ox heart (page **144**) and minute steaks. Things cook and burn very quickly in this zone and require constant tending.

ZONE 3

No longer cooking directly over charcoal, but still quite hot. Fat is much prized at **BAM** but requires a touch more time to cook through than the meat takes to reach temperature, so cooking a fatty cut demands a level of attention. This less aggressive cooking area reduces the risk of flare ups when grilling any fatty meat that needs to render first. Anything that will leach fat that will ignite the coals will cook well here. This is why I tend to cook Adana Skewers (page **142**) in this zone.

ZONE 1

ZONE 3

ZONE 4

ZONE 2

ZONE 2

Moving a little to the right, there is an area that is half directly over the coals, and half not. This is where we tend to flame grill thicker steaks, and also to achieve satisfying bar marks on fish and small birds. The escaping meat juices produce wisps of smoke that flavour the meat in a way that you don't get in a pan or on a gas barbecue. The majority of the grilled vegetables like hispi cabbage (page **107**) and sweetcorn (page **108**) are started in this zone to achieve a decent char but not get incinerated, before moving to a cooler zone to cook through.

ZONE 4

This zone still produces a decent amount of heat and is ideal to carry a piece of meat or a fish though to its desired temperature. It's also good for refreshing pre-cooked flatbreads.

GRILLING METHOD

For those not used to the grilling process, I've written a step-by-step method that will guide you in the right direction. I say guide, because that is exactly what this is – a guide, not an exact method. If you have little or no experience with grilling, or even cooking, my suggestion is to get organized. Have all your ingredients ready, tongs handy and plates to put the cooked meat on. It's hard to concentrate if you give yourself too much to do in too little time, and by doing so you reduce your ability to observe and learn anything about the process, other than it's really stressful and you weren't happy with anything you cooked and now all your friends hate you because they are hangry. Well, guess what? They already didn't like you... but they might have liked you more or at least pretended to like you if you grilled food like a total slayer. Self esteem is a great motivation to get good at cooking, and cooking well will win you friends. I have way more friends now than I did before I could cook, and I definitely got luckier with the ladies. That's the way to win – get good at something most people don't have a flare for or think is too difficult to achieve, when it really isn't. Trust me, if I can do it you can – it's all about understanding the variables that come with cooking. This takes time and practice, which ultimately means you will spend a few quid on ingredients in doing so, but if cooking really flicks your switch then it's money well spent.

So with that in mind, when it comes to grilling, it's important to start with something simple. Any person in their right mind loves short ribs. You can marinade them in many ways, they cook quickly and need little resting time. Familiarize yourself with the cooking zones (page 43) before doing this.

GRILLED KOREAN SHORT RIBS

I actually chuckled at how quick and easy these ribs were to cook, and how good they were to eat. I invest a lot of time testing and honing the flavours and process for something like the Lamb Offal Flatbread (page 160), so when I find an ingredient like these ribs that require very little effort and offer fantastic results I get excited and resentful in equal measures. Korean short ribs are not something I would attempt to cut myself, so ask your butcher to do this.

2 kg/4½ lb Korean-style aged short rib, 1–1.5 cm (½ –¾ in) thickness, about 12 in total
salt
50 g (2 oz/½ stick) butter, melted
fish sauce
best quality soy sauce you can access

1/2/3
First, get the barbecue ripping hot.

4
In a mixing bowl or roasting pan, generously salt the short ribs. Have a separate roasting pan with the melted butter ready to rest the cooked ribs in.

5
On a standard-sized barbecue, I like to grill the ribs in batches of about four at a time so I can tend each one easily and have enough space on the grill to combat flare ups. Char the ribs on one side in zone 1 for 2–3 minutes.

6
Once done, flip the ribs, season and char hard again for 3–4 minutes. If the ribs are causing flare up or are taking on too much colour, move to a cooler part of the grill to finish. I have never used a temperature probe on short ribs cooked this way – if the meat is charred and chestnut brown and the fat softened, they are ready.

7

Put the first batch of ribs in the roasting pan with the butter and a splash of fish sauce while you cook the rest, repeating with every batch. Cut each rib into four, each piece possessing a segment of bone, providing a cute little nugget to grasp when eating.

8

Pile the ribs on a plate. Add a big splash of soy sauce to the butter in the pan and pour it over the short ribs.

ON BARBECUES

TIPS FROM MARK 'LORD LOGS' PARR

I consulted my good friend and pyro oracle Mark Parr of the London Log Company to see if he had any realistic suggestions as to how to improve a home barbecue and set up the coals properly with little effort. I was expecting a few tips via text maybe, but instead I received the most eloquent of emails. Here's what he said:

Most retail barbecues lack any kind of fundamental insulation; it's often bulky and heavy to add to a standard off-the-shelf bit of kit, so understandably manufacturers avoid it. However, the rise of ceramic Kamado-style barbecues shows the benefit of being able to control the heat with insulation in a long cook, and to do so this type uses expensive, NASA-like ceramic.

For home cooking, heat retention is just as precious, and this fundamental method is invaluable, even if you've not laid out good money on one of these appliances.

If you own a drum or kettle-style barbecue, it can be upgraded with a simple layer of sharp sand (often sold as plasterers' sand) if you so wish. Sand is one of nature's super insulators – it's easy to work with, safe and cheap. Buy a bag at your local DIY shop or friendly builders' merchant.

Consider what you're trying to achieve by adding a base of sand into the appliance. If you imagine when a fire is set in the drum or kettle, the heat dissipation goes two ways: up towards the food, because heat rises, but also outwards as radiant heat as the appliance gets hotter. Now, imagine if you could contain some of the radiant heat into one slab in the base of the kettle or grill, and use that heat to stabilize the cooking process and reduce the actual amount of fuel you use. Sand takes a long time to release its energy once hot, and this is the benefit you're looking for.

Simply add a layer of sand as deep as you can into the base – you can always take some away as you see fit. In a drum-style barbecue, you'll get about 7.5 cm (3 inches) in the deepest part – you'll instantly notice the difference in the way the drum performs. On a kettle-style barbecue you can pack it down and then craft the sand away from the vents to allow air flow – it'll take a little practice, but it is satisfying once mastered.

Once the sand is in, tamp it down evenly to compress it. You'll need to set a 'curing' fire to drive off the moisture held in the sand before you cook for the first time (it often holds quite a lot). To do this, burn the usual amount of charcoal in your barbecue – about an hour or two should do it. Allow it to cool well for a good few hours then poke a skewer into the sand for a few moments – it should now be cool, dry and ready to start cooking on. Also make sure you cover the appliance from the rain, with the lid on, preferably under a barbecue cover. We do this for all of our appliances at events and festivals and we reckon we save about 30 per cent on the fuel, so less stock to transport. There's also the added bonus of the way it protects the steel appliance, as direct heat and wood ash can corrode the steel fairly quickly. The sand lessens this corrosion, and as I write this I'm getting why the makers don't give this tip out.

A FEW THINGS WORTH NOTING

The sand-filled appliance performs better over a longer period, but it does require a little more time to fire up initially, as you have to warm the sand up as you start. The benefits will be obvious once it gets going, so run with it.

Technique-wise, I pile the coals into a dome and add natural fire lighters into the top of the coals, as a charcoal fire burns upside-down, as it were, so the smoke from the charcoal underneath has to pass through the hot surface layer and this secondary burn cleans the smoke, so you get a nice clear fire. Once lit and the all white-grey ash has formed, I then spread the coals to my right and add a few more at this point, if required.

I generally cook off-set (see page 43) – that is hot coals to my right, then an indirect space to rest the food over, and here's where the sand plays its part. As the sand heats up, it radiates into the whole cook area and allows you to keep the food a little away from the vigour of the fire, to cook slowly in the heat without burning. Of course you want all the benefits of the fire-char and to add colour to the meat and vegetables, or even fruits. But with the lid down, you're creating more of an oven effect, and this heat stability greatly improves the outcomes of most dishes.

It's also good to sit things in the barbecue for a low and slow cook after the faster cooking has been done. Do use a temperature probe to make sure all the meat is safe, but fish and veg will love this way of low and slow heat, as the fires dies down and the sand gives out its heat – you've paid for it and put the time and effort in, so best put it to good use.

SMOKING

Smoking is the next in the Holy Trinity of techniques at Black Axe Mangal.

The electric smoker at **BAM** still technically belongs to Tom Adams, the founder of Pitt Cue, who now lives and cooks at his smallholding, Coombeshead Farm, in Cornwall. After peppering Tom with texts and emails about smoking, he 'lent' me his tiny Cookshack Electric smoker in a bid to shut me up. That was many years ago now, and unfortunately for him, the texts and emails haven't stopped.

The smoker is essentially a very basic oven with a hole in the top, controlled by a crude element that accommodates a smoke box. When you put wood in the smoke box and turn it on, the element heats up, the wood combusts, and smoke makes its way up and out through the hole in the top, dancing around whatever you have in there. Our smoker reaches a maximum temperature of **120°C/250°F**, and can go as low as **50°C/120°F**. We also use it to cook joints of meat or terrines at low temperatures when we aren't using it as a smoker.

Smoking indoors in an electric smoker is as simple as it gets. The biggest advantages of an electric smoker are its ability to maintain a constant temperature, and that it requires very little interference. It is by far the simplest way to hot smoke food that I know of, once you become familiar with a few variables.

It might be easier and more consistent, but there is definitely something less romantic about using an electric smoker, and I'm grateful my enthusiasm for smoking meat encouraged me to explore and experiment with other smoking methods and techniques before I went electric – I've given you step-by-step methods for flash smoking, smoking in a barbecue and making a **DIY** fire pit in this section, should you want to experiment. The most primitive of these methods is the fire pit, which I first made after spontaneously digging a hole in my back garden and lining it with paving slabs and a few bricks. That pit was a lot of fun – it cost fuck all and I got some decent results for someone who didn't have a clue what they were doing. It was great for cooking large casseroles over the course of the day, and it produced the best smoked chicken I've ever managed to cook. I made use of it most weekends until Kate and the kids decided I needed an upgrade and bought me a Kadai fire bowl for my birthday.

WOOD SELECTION

If you're hot smoking meat for long periods of time, you can't go wrong with good ol' fashioned dry woods such as cherry, apple and oak, which can flavour your meat in different ways. Pine, cedar and other soft wood can impart a bitter smoke. It goes without saying, but avoid any woods that have been treated (like pallets), because Christ knows what will end up transferring onto the food.

The woods we use at BAM are oak, cherry, silver birch, apple and sweet chestnut. I don't discriminate or have a personal favourite. For a six-hour smoke we use roughly 100 g/3½ oz of wood.

OAK

Extremely versatile, with a classic medium to heavy smoke. Works with just about any meat, vegetables or fish we smoke at the restaurant, with the added bonus of being readily available.

SILVER BIRCH

Less common, with a sweet and round flavour on the smoke that lends itself well to fish. It's also surprisingly good with aged beef.

SWEET CHESTNUT

Use this in the same way as the silver birch, but you'll need to add another chunk or two if you're smoking for a longer period as it burns faster.

CHERRY

Lighter than oak but still a decent all-rounder, cherry wood marries well with pork and poultry. I've used it to smoke our cherry purée because I like the romantic notion. We stoke the smoker with a little more cherry wood to lock in the flavour. It works very well with duck and mallard (wild duck).

APPLE

In my experience, apple is the strongest of the fruit woods. I think it goes well with everything and will use it constantly if we have it in at **BAM**. The smoke also burns a pleasing light blue.

HARVESTING AND SELECTING HERBS AND TWIGS FOR SMOKING

These can be harvested from your garden, someone else's garden, the park... wherever this sort of thing grows. I find that I rarely have use for a whole bunch of thyme I've bought from the supermarket. It can be used to smoke something on the barbecue or stuffed inside a bird to influence its cooking juices. For hay, I generally buy a massive bag from the pet shop and it lasts indefinitely. I will also run over to the park every now and again and snip some cherry or chestnut twigs when the ranger isn't looking. It's not like I'm felling trees though – if I was allowed I would have deforested half of Wanstead Flats by now. Have you ever chopped a tree down with an axe? It's pretty primal. I digress. These twigs and herbs can be combined to make a cocktail of flavours, and their varying degrees of size and decay will determine the smoke time.

HAY

Hay provides instant and brief combustion. Slightly green hay has a better flavour and marginally slower burn than the totally dry stuff. This works well for the flash smoking method (page 48) or smoking seafood or shellfish over coals in a perforated frying pan. Not to be confused with straw, which isn't much good for smoking.

ROSEMARY

The resin in fresh rosemary can be a little on the bitter side when burnt; branches that have dried for a few days or have been taken from a dying plant are ideal. Rosemary stems ignite slower than hay and thyme, but still pretty fast. The larger branches from bigger bushes burn slower and give a pleasant layer of smoke to whatever you are smoking. I suggest combining with a sweet wood like apple or chestnut for a rounder flavour.

FENNEL STEMS

The stems, or twigs, as I call them, are the best bit of the vegetable. I like fennel, but I find everything above the bulb more interesting. I first came across them at St. JOHN, where Fergus uses fennel twigs to stuff and roast sea bass, giving the delicate fish and the cooking juices a terrific aroma and flavour. And it's the scent that I value so highly. I later discovered if you pile a few pencil-sized twigs next to a fish on a grill and cover that with a cloche,

it gives the fish a decent lick of smoke (see page 48). I've struggled over the years to buy fennel twigs. There was a decent Egyptian supply for a while but that went dry, so I rely on keen, kind-hearted gardeners to facilitate my habits now.

THYME TWIGS

A sweet fragrance with small tinder for quick ignition. Similar to hay in its uses, but also good to use in combination with apple, cherry or oak for a slower burn.

BAY BRANCHES

Give a strong, spicy, aromatic and sweet aroma, much like the flavour bay leaves impart when added to a stock or roasted inside a chicken. Full of complex oils that will produce notes of clove and menthol. Allow to dry for a spell, and use sparingly.

HOTBOXING, OR FLASH SMOKING

Hotboxing, or flash smoking, is a combination of grilling and smoking. It's a fun way to get a lick of smoke on small birds, fish or vegetables – anything that doesn't take that long to cook. The theory behind this technique is the same as if you're smoking weed in a car with all the windows up, hence the name. If you pile a few pencil-sized fennel twigs and a couple of balls of hay next to a fillet of fish on a grill and cover that with the barbecue lid, the fish flash smokes. This method might be called something else somewhere else, but flash smoked is what I've always called it. I used to use fennel twigs exclusively, but when they ran out I turned to other trees and plants and my options increased – see page 47 for some ideas.

HOTBOX MACKEREL

ESSENTIAL EQUIPMENT

barbecue (see page 43) with lid or cloche
tongs
10–12 fennel twigs, roughly pencil sized
4 bay leaves
large handful of hay, rolled into tight balls

SERVES 2-4

2 whole mackerel, or 4 fillets
1 teaspoon vegetable or sunflower oil
sea salt flakes
50 g (2 oz/½ stick) butter, melted

—
1
Fire up the barbecue using the off-set technique (page 43).

—
2
Lay the mackerel on a plate and rub the skin lightly all over with the oil. Season with sea salt flakes on either side.

—
3/4
Have the fennel twigs, bay and hay ready. Hold your hand over the barbecue and decide where the best spot is to cook your mackerel. You're looking for a medium heat, so closer to the cooler third of it. Lay your fish on the barbecue. Immediately place the twigs, bay and hay down on the grill about 7.5 cm (3 inches) away from the fish.

—
5/6/7
When the twigs and bay catch fire add the hay. Ignite the hay then cover the barbecue with the lid, or a cloche if you don't have a lid. This should extinguish the flames, but leave sufficient air flow to allow the twigs and hay to smoke.

—
8/9/10

Cook for **3–4 minutes**. Remove the cloche or lid, flip the fish, replace the lid and cook for a further **3–4 minutes**. After this time it should be blistered and golden. If it's looking good gently transfer the fish to a roasting pan, skin-side up, and add the butter.

—
11/12

Put the pan on the cooler third of the barbecue to finish cooking the mackerel. This step will also infuse the butter with the smokiness of the mackerel. This should take **2–3 minutes**. I like to throw in some sea greens at the end, too.

SMOKING IN AN ELECTRIC SMOKER

For me, the hardest part of using an electric smoker was keeping the smoker door shut, something I found impossible to do at first. I kept opening the door to check whatever I had in there, and almost always put way too much wood in, resulting in smoke alarms sounding during service. If you keep the door shut and don't overload it with wood, you are halfway there. Once you work out the ideal internal temperature each cut has to get to, and how long it takes to hit that sweet spot, you're almost all the way there. We use a Cookshack smoker at BAM, but have a look online to find what's right for you.

Variables will always be a factor. Climate, the size and weight of the meat, and how much you've crammed into the smoker will all affect cooking times. This sounds obvious but I'm going to say it anyway – the more you use your smoker the easier it is to recognize these variables and take them into account. Some people like to put a pan of water in to keep the meat moist. I've never really done this other than the few times I've smoked a brisket all the way in the smoker. If the smoker is mostly full, I find that it's never really short on moisture.

BAM BACON

We cure the bellies we get from the middles of pork delivered to the restaurant, but I appreciate that at home, you might not have the relative luxury of a walk-in refrigerator that you can store and cure a whole belly in for a week. The cure can be scaled down according to the size of the belly. Nice thick plastic containers are handy for this, or alternatively you can mummify the belly in cling film (plastic wrap) and leave it in a tray. Try leaving the bones on as we do... one of my greatest pleasures is gnawing on a rib with greasy fingers, especially if you've cured, hung, smoked and cooked the pork yourself. We leave the skin on and smoke the belly skin-side down to protect the meat from taking on too hard a smoke. People cure in lots of different ways, but making bacon this way works for us. Once the bacon is smoked, it is essentially cooked and will eat like gammon, so can be shaved and consumed cold, cut and grilled, or cut into chunks and fried until crispy.

ESSENTIAL EQUIPMENT

electric smoker
gastronorm or very large pan
sharp boning knife
butcher's hook or string
digital thermometer

MAKES 5 KG (11 LB)

5 kg/11 lb fatty pork belly with skin, fat and ribs attached
sunflower oil
100 g (3½ oz/½ cup) fine salt
100 g (3½ oz/½ cup) demerara sugar
2 tablespoons saltpeter (potassium nitrate; optional)
5 tablespoons Bakken Spice (page 197)

1
I like to keep as much fat on my bacon as possible but if there is an excessive amount of fat on the rib side of the belly, even it up by cutting a little off. This will improve the chances of an even cure.

–

2
There is a membrane-type skin that covers the ribs and the belly fat. Do your best to remove this as it can be stubborn to come off once cooked and tends to burn when grilling. Tease a little of the skin off the bottom of a rib with a knife until you can grip it between your finger and thumb and gently pull. Sometimes this membrane comes off in one satisfying strip, other times in annoying scraps.

5
Place in a gastronorm or a pan big enough to accommodate it comfortably, and leave in the refrigerator overnight, or for around 12 hours. After that period, flip the belly every day for the next 5 days. Five days is a good rule of thumb to check how your belly is progressing. Have a feel of the belly; the thickness of the belly will dictate the length of time it spends in the cure. We get some seriously fatty pigs in at times and the fact that we leave bones and skin on tends to lead to a longer curing period. If your belly feels firm for the most part, though, it's ready to hang. If it feels a little soft put it back in the refrigerator for another day or two. The salty liquid that gathers at the bottom of the container is enough to continue to cure the belly if you're flipping daily.

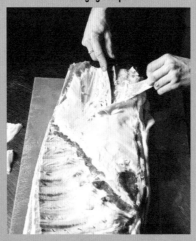

3/4
Stab both the skin and flesh sides of the pork all over with a sharp boning knife, being careful not to go the whole way through. With a touch of oil, mix the salt, sugar, saltpeter and Bakken Spice together in a small bowl, then apply the mix to the belly.

When you're ready to smoke the belly, place it skin-side down in an electric smoker (cut it in half if you need to). Follow the manufacturer's instructions and set it between **100-110°C/210-230°F**. Smoke the belly until it reaches an internal temperature of **76-79°C/168-175°F**. This will take a few hours at least. A digital probe is the best way to judge this accurately.

—
11

Once cooked, rest for a minimum of **30-45 minutes**. If you've timed dinner to perfection and are keen to serve it hot out the smoker, remove the skin (this is full of flavour so keep this to add to stocks and sauces) pressing the sharp of the knife tight to the skin, leaving as much fat on the belly as possible, and slice into finger-width slabs from the fatty end.

—
6/7

When the belly is ready to hang, rinse lightly with cold water, pat dry and hang on a butcher's hook or with string in a dry part of the refrigerator for a further **2-5 days**. That might not be so easy in a conventional refrigerator. The way I've tackled this in the past is laying the meat on a rack set into a pan allowing the air to circulate around the meat, flipping it daily.

—
12

If you want to cut a bacon 'chop' go in at the rib end and simply flip the belly and cut along the ribs. A sharp carving knife is pretty much essential. Keep your slices looking pretty by using the whole of the knife in a long cutting motion when carving. If you're planning on eating it later, cool completely, wrap in cling film (plastic wrap) and refrigerate. Use within **5 days**.

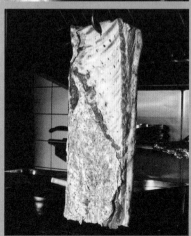

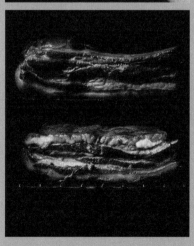

SMOKING IN A KETTLE BARBECUE

What type of barbecue do you have? Is it an all singing, all dancing ceramic egg-type thing? A drum or a kettle barbecue? The quality and condition of your equipment will determine how easy or difficult it is to smoke food successfully, but the actual principles for smoking are the same across the board.

The rise of online shops means you can conveniently order whatever you need and have it delivered to your door. There are lots of options and outlets to buy a whole range of charcoal, fire lighters and all the barbecue paraphernalia you could ever need. Fuel wise, there are lots of options and varying degrees of quality.

However, for the purpose of this book – knowing what most people already have at home – I used a bog-standard kettle barbecue with a digital thermometer and readily available charcoal. I wanted to get a realistic sense of how achievable this method is for a keen home cook using the most basic equipment, and was curious to work out the pros and cons for each type of fuel available on the market.

Simply put, if you buy cheap charcoal it will burn super quick, require frequent topping up and monitoring of temperature, especially if you are using a thin metal kettle barbecue. I've had great results cooking this way, and I'm sure you can too, but the process is more hassle and the variables I alluded to above play a much bigger role. Weather is a big consideration. I tried this method in the height of summer and the dead of winter. It took nearly twice as long to smoke four large pig jowls between 100–110ºC/210–230ºF in the winter, consumed more fuel, and needed topping up at regular intervals. This process will take practice to master and it isn't a case of putting something on a barbecue and walking away for hours to come back and find a perfectly smoked piece of meat. In conclusion, smoking on crude equipment is time demanding, but totally doable. You'll need to engage and observe what is going on to get the best results. I would recommend investing in long-burning fuel such as compressed sawdust charcoal if you want an easier ride. This type of fuel will offer little in flavour but will provide a much longer, more even

and consistent heat, which will need less tending when smoking food. The flavour will come from the wood you select for smoking. The higher quality your barbecue, the easier it is to maintain the desired temperature, but you still need to commit to get decent results.

The aim is to maintain a temperature between 100–120ºC/210–250ºF. My ideal temperature for smoking is 110ºC/230ºF.

Have all your equipment and utensils close to hand and ready to go. Make sure your barbecue is free of any spent coals and the grill has received a good going over with a wire brush. I like to dab a touch of oil on a rag and give the grill a little wipe to lift off any rust.

It might be an idea to put a pan under the barbecue to catch any escaping fat that renders out of the meat.

PREPARING YOUR BARBECUE FOR SMOKING

Apart from wood and charcoal (obvs) and a barbecue, you will need a metal pan that fits well inside the barbecue, or an old roasting pan that you don't care about ruining, and a digital instant-read thermometer.

I found this method for how to smoke pig's cheeks scribbled on a stained scrap of paper in the back of a notebook. It's definitely my scrawl, but I don't remember writing it... seems legit though, and this is how we do it still.

SMOKED PIG'S CHEEKS

ESSENTIAL EQUIPMENT

barbecue (see page 43)
roasting pan
digital thermometer
60-100 g/2-3½ oz wood (see page 47)

MAKES 3-6

vegetable oil
3 x large or 6 x small pig's cheeks (jowls),
700-900 g/1½-2 lb each, skin on
4-6 cloves garlic, minced
1 tablespoon Bakken Spice (page 197)
200 g/7 oz (½ cup) 50/50 sea salt and caster
(superfine) sugar mix

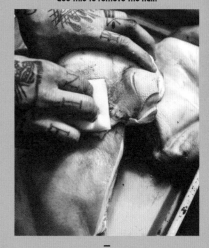

–
1
First clean the pig's cheeks.
If you have a blow torch,
use this to remove the hair.

–
2/3
Lightly oil the pig's cheeks to help the spice and the garlic adhere to the meat. Rub the garlic and Bakken on the flesh side, then cover the jowls with 50/50 salt and sugar. You can smoke the cheeks straight after rubbing but I think the cheeks benefit from a day or two in the refrigerator at this stage if you have the time and space do it.

Smoke the meat, rotating once or
twice, until it has reached an internal temperature
of **78–80°C/172–176°F.**

–
4

Open the vents in the bottom of the barbecue.
Place about **3** cupped handfuls of charcoal
on one side on the bottom grill. Lay **4–6** lumps
of long burning, compressed charcoal on top of that.
Nestle a natural fire lighter or two between
the long burners then add another cupped
handful or two of charcoal on top. Light
the fire lighters, then let the fire burn down.
Put the roasting pan next to the coals and
fill it to the brim with water.

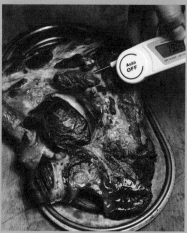

–
7

During winter, I use a chimney starter to top
up the charcoal when the temperature dips below
100°C/210°F. Follow the manufacturer's
instructions to prepare the starter. If the
temperature drops, top up the charcoal with
the coals from the starter by lifting the grill.
Add a little at a time to prevent the grill from
getting too hot.

–
10

Remove the cheeks and chill. A flat tray
in a sink full of ice can speed up this process.
Refrigerate until the cheeks are completely chilled.
At this stage, you can remove the skin, cut the
cheek into **2.5 cm (1 inch)** pieces, then fry in a little
oil until crispy and gold, or follow the Pig's Cheek
and Prune Doughnuts recipe on **page 98.**
You won't want to eat the skin, so you can either
discard it or use it for flavouring stocks.

–
5/6

Place the lid on with the thermometer over the
cooler half. I do this to gauge the temperature
in the area that I want place the meat – if you put
the thermometer directly over or too close to the
heat, you will get a higher and inaccurate temperature
reading. If the temperature is anywhere between
110–130°C/230–270°F close the bottom vents
almost all the way. Lift the grill off the barbecue and
reheap the coals into a pile snug against the wall
of the barbecue. Put your chosen smoking wood on top
of the coals. Replace the grill. Arrange the cheeks on
the grill over the water pan then replace the lid making
sure the thermometer is above the meat. Open the vent
on the lid a crack to encourage the air flow.

DIY FIRE PIT

Here is a loose description of how to make your own fire pit in your back garden. Make sure you get permission from the garden owner first.

Materials are simple – you just need surplus house bricks, building blocks or paving slabs, and a shovel.

Dig a hole that's roughly 1 x 1 x 1 m (40 x 40 x 40 inch) preferably away from any tree or plant root systems that make digging a hole even more laborious. Level the bottom of the hole the best you can. Lay a paving slab in the bottom of the hole. Alternatively, line it with bricks. If you have more paving slabs available, use these to line the sides. If not, stack bricks around the edge of the hole as you would lay bricks when building a wall. It's worth taking a bit of time getting this right to reduce the chances of collapse. Find something that can be laid over the pit such as a piece of plywood. Pile coals into the hole, then light with a fire lighter or blow torch. And that's it.

I started cooking meat over coals using skewers and sticks, and then tried grilling mussels and shellfish on wire mesh – whatever I had laying around the garden or in my shed, I made use of. There was something deeply satisfying about the whole set-up. It took a while for the penny to drop, but I eventually realized that I could achieve a decent level of smoke by laying splints of wood over the fading coals. I actually cite a happy accident with a chicken as a turning point that helped me understand the most fundamental principles of how smoke behaves. I let the fire burn down too much (or what I thought was too much), and then as Kate and I had to go out with the kids, I spatchcocked a chicken, seasoned it with salt and placed it skin-side down over the embers on an old cake rack. I threw a few fennel twigs and a couple of cherry branches on the coals, covered the pit with a piece of plywood to keep the crows away and just left it. When we came back a couple of hours later, neither Kate nor I could believe how well the chicken had cooked, and how good the smoke was. I tried to replicate the process, but the results were never quite as special. There are obviously many variables here, and it will be trial and error, but if you have the inclination to build a pit, the ultimate smoked chicken is worth pursuing.

FIRE PIT SMOKED CHICKEN

ESSENTIAL EQUIPMENT

fire pit (see left)
wire rack
tongs
digital thermometer

SERVES 4

8-10 large chicken thighs, skin on
sea salt

1/2
Get the coals burning in your fire pit, and wait for them to die down to glowing embers. Add any aromatics you have to hand (see page 47).

3/4
Once the coals are at a low heat, salt the thighs and place them over a rack that sits just above the coals in your fire pit, skin-side down, then cover with plywood or whatever you have to hand. Leave to cook through (they can take up to two hours), but try not to lift the lid too frequently.

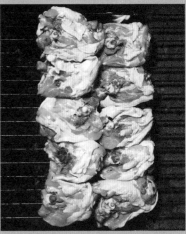

5/6/7
Check the chicken occasionally, turning it over towards the end of the cooking time. The chicken is done when the juices run clear from the legs or the internal temperature measures 75°C/165°F on a digital probe.

—
8
Serve straight away with your favourite accompaniments, or use in the Smoked Chicken Caesar Salad, below.

SMOKED CHICKEN CAESAR SALAD

You don't have to smoke the chicken thighs... but there is nothing complicated about smoking chicken thighs or whole chickens on a barbecue or in a fire pit (see left), and it's a very approachable intro-duction to smoking for any novice. The crispy cheese element negates the need to use croutons in this salad, but if you're a traditionalist, fry a few chunks of decent bread or leftover BAM Flatbread (pages 58–62) and throw them in. Crispy cheese is a nice addition to any salad or soup – I especially like it on butternut squash soup. The cheese will keep for a few days in an airtight container.

SERVES 4-6

sunflower oil, for frying
100 g/3½ oz Gubbeen or Parmesan cheese, very finely grated
8–10 chicken thighs, skin on, smoked (see left)
2 Cos lettuce, leaves separated and roughly torn
2 tablespoons Lemon Oil (page 198)
1 teaspoon grape must mustard or wholegrain mustard
1 x quantity Anchovy Dressing (page 198)

1
Preheat the oven to 80°C/175°F/Gas Mark ¼.

—
2
Secure a sheet of baking (parchment) paper to a baking sheet with a touch of oil. Scatter the cheese over every available space on the sheet – try not to clump the cheese together as it won't crisp up. Bake until crispy with a hint of colour, about 8–10 minutes. Allow to cool.

—
3
Debone the chicken thighs and chop each into 6–8 pieces. If you have opted to smoke the chicken ahead of time, and so chilled in the refrigerator, fry the thigh meat in a little oil in a non-stick frying pan over a medium low heat, skin-side down. Once the skin is crispy, around 10–12 minutes, flip and finish cooking. Remove from the heat and let the chicken rest under foil while you prepare the rest of the salad, whether it's just out of the pan or just finished smoking.

—
4
Toss the lettuce with the Lemon Oil and mustard in a large bowl. Fold in the chicken and toss with the Anchovy Dressing. Spoon the salad onto a serving platter, crumble the crisp cheese over the top and serve.

BREAD

To quote food writer Richard Olney, bread is the 'symbol of sustenance', and I couldn't agree more. The bread we make at **BAM** is, and always will be, a fundamental facet of our identity. Originally **Black Axe Mangal** was going to be a kebab shop stroke Turkish mangal (barbecue), and for a very short period of time, it kinda was. Our food and attitude has evolved to such an extent that it is hard to pigeonhole our cuisine, but I would say that bread is the anchor. The 'true north' of **BAM**.

I remember my disappointment when my regular kebab haunts transitioned from pita bread to thin tortilla wraps. The pita was always a bit shit, but the tortilla just fell apart and made it a total mess to eat, diminishing the pleasure I got from my doner. This didn't slow down my kebab consumption, but it did bring me to the conclusion that the bread is pivotal and as important as what it is wrapped around.

Tas Firin on Bethnal Green Road in East London is a good example of this. They make all the bread served at the restaurant in a wood-fired oven (if you are looking for a killer Adana kebab, get yourself down to Tas, or order a lahmacun, a type of thin Turkish bread with toppings, that will come with a salad and order an Adana to eat with it). At lunch and at quieter times, I noticed that they sometimes cook the bread to order, which accentuates the flavours of the grilled meats and dips. This reinforced my thoughts on bread being key, and became the catalyst for my obsession. Making good bread and serving it with grilled meats.

I have Chad Robertson to thank for **BAM**'s flatbread recipe. The first time I met Chad and tried Tartine bread was at Mission Chinese Food when it was still on Orchard Street in New York. Danny (in true Danny Bowien style) had dozens of loaves shipped from San Francisco to New York for an Edible Selby dinner that we were cooking 'breakfast' dishes for. A combination of Meat Hook tank-cured bacon (they call it Canadian bacon in the US), St. JOHN tomato ketchup and Tartine bread made the best bacon sarnie ever. After this, I'd fantasized hard about Tartine bread, so when I went to San Francisco and had the chance to try it at source, I was beyond excited. Chad was scoring and loading the loaves into the oven when I arrived; we drank coffee and chatted while the bread was baking. Chad is a very mellow guy, which is reflected in his baking style. I'd mentioned my concept to Chad before and his enthusiasm for the idea gave me confidence. I'd also mentioned my inability to nail a decent flatbread, which he said Tartine could help with. We retrieved

the loaves from the oven together using welder's gloves. The aroma from the sesame loaf was particularly intoxicating. Waiting for those loaves to cool enough to cut was agonizing. Chad cut and buttered a slice for me. That slice of bread permanently changed my perception and expectation of what bread can be, in the same way Fergus' bone marrow and Danny's chicken wings had changed my perception and expectation of food. While I was digesting this moment, Chad handed me a recipe for a dough that he thought would work as a flatbread – I was stumped that one of the world's greatest bakers would be so generous with his knowledge. For this I am forever grateful – the gift of this dough is the foundation of Black Axe Mangal. Chad did go on to explain how to make the bread, but I didn't take any notes. I thought I'd remember how to make the dough, but when I returned to the UK I had predictably been unable to retain the information and forgotten. Luckily while I was at Tartine, I had also met Richard Hart, who was the head baker (now of Hart Bageri, Copenhagen). Richard hails from Leyton, East London, which is just down the road from me and Kate, and despite living in San Francisco for years, Richard had lost none of his London twang. We became mates for life on the spot.

A couple of weeks before the pop-up in Copenhagen was due to start, I was ready to throw in the towel and cancel the entire project. I couldn't get the flatbread right. Why the fuck didn't I pay attention to Chad and write anything down? I got in touch with Rich about the dough. He sent me a text saying he would be in England the week before we left for Copenhagen, and would come and show me how to make the bread. 'Don't worry about it man'. He also reassured me that I didn't need any fancy mixers or dough-rolling machines, 'just some starter and a big bucket or plastic tub is all we need'.

True to his word, Richard came over, we had a cup of tea and he showed me how to make the dough. Rich weighed all the ingredients out in a plastic bowl, mixed them by hand and requested another cup of tea. I put the kettle on. Rich went on to explain the variables you have to consider when making dough, and that the variables dictate how long the dough will take to make and how it will turn out. We folded the dough by hand twice more and had another cuppa – Rich drinks a lot of tea. After the third turn, we put the dough in the refrigerator to chill a bit. 'That's it mate, now you just grill it.' I was stunned. This dough was the least stressful method I'd ever come across, but that is the Tartine ultra-zen style. We grilled the bread and dipped it in smoked mutton fat. It was exactly what I'd been striving for.

A NOTE ON PIZZA OVENS

My wife Kate and I built a huge Alan Scott-style bread oven in our back garden some years ago. We wanted an oven that we could bake multiple sourdough loaves in, and had this romantic idea that we would indulge our passion for bread on our days off and give a few loaves away to the neighbours while we were at it. A naive notion in retrospect, but one I hope to achieve in the future. I love that oven like I love my own children, but I don't get to play with it nearly enough nowadays. Chopping the logs with an axe, stacking them just so, trying to light the fire using just one match and kindling might all sound Neolithic to some, but I get off on it every time, and it never feels like work.

I know this oven well now, but the first time I attempted to cook something in it was a complete disaster. After weeks of planning, building and emotional investment, the moment came to actually use the oven, and I was beyond excitement. To mark the occasion, we decided to cook pizza together as a family. In my mind, the pizza we were about to make in this oven was going to be the absolute best pizza we had ever tasted – the best pizza the world had ever tasted. I visualized the moment where we all fell silent after our first bite and shared that 'look' followed by a slight sigh, and lightning passing through me and lifting my exalted body into the sky like Connor MacLeod's 'quickening' when he receives The Prize in *Highlander*. My children would worship me, my wife would love me for all eternity, and I would become immortal.

In reality, the first pizza stuck to the peel, spilling most of the cheese into the flames. Not to worry, I thought; with a fair amount of persuasion and extra flour the base was freed, re-topped and loaded back into the oven, where it combusted upon contact and fused itself to the oven floor. I can still see the disappointed looks on my sons' faces, followed by the inevitable question: 'Is that supposed to happen, Dad?', while I frantically tried to retrieve the incinerated pizza from the flames. I was crushed and felt utterly pathetic. In my blind enthusiasm, I'd loaded way too much wood into the oven – I could have smelted lead in the bloody thing.

I had to wait until the dough fully carbonized (which didn't take long at that temperature) before I could sweep the debris clear and try again. We ate okay pizza that night. My enthusiasm had evaporated, I had zero sense of humour left, and I was too grumpy to just enjoy the moment with my family, which disappointed my children more than not eating the best pizza the world has ever tasted. What I'd built up in my head to be a life-changing event manifested into a petulant, stressful horror show. I sulked about it for days after, and my kids haven't let me forget about it, either.

The most important line in any cookbook ever is written is in Fergus Henderson's *Nose to Tail Eating: A Kind of British Cooking*. 'Don't be afraid of cooking as your ingredients will know and misbehave. Enjoy your cooking and the food will behave; moreover it will pass your pleasure onto those that eat it.' This is where I have to ask you to use some common sense. I'm pretty confident I've never been to your house, so there is no way I have any intimate knowledge of where the hot spots are in your oven, how long it takes to get to temperature or how quickly it cools down, what fuel you're using and so on. You have to take a little responsibility and initiative here. If you think this is a cop out on my part for not providing you with an exact set of temperatures and times that will give you the perfect product every time, then I suggest you buy yourself a microwave oven, plug it in, follow the instructions on the package and enjoy a romantic meal for one.

FLATBREAD

This is the most basic of breads, and the easiest to pat out and cook on a barbecue, which is still my favourite and preferred method. I love watching the bubbles and ridges form across the surface of the bread on contact with extreme heat. Those bubbles and ridges char wonderfully when turned. The char gives the bread a varied texture and an incredible flavour.

All dough products are sensitive to their environment, so working in extremes is not ideal. Too cold and dough will take an age to rise or develop. Likewise, a hot environment excoriates the process. It's worth investing in a decent quality plastic, see-through container with a tight fitting lid. This will insulate the dough and give you a visual indication of its development and health. You'll need to take the tub size into consideration and ask yourself how much dough you will feasibly be making. You don't want to be emptying out your refrigerator every time you make bread. Whatever quantity of dough you're making, it's safe to say that it will at least double in size when proved. Smaller batches will rise in the suggested time, but if you double the quantity, bear in mind that it may take more time.

Poolish is a type of bread starter that is often used as an alternative to a traditional sourdough starter, and can be made spontaneously if you're eager to get a batch of flatbreads on the go. If you have a healthy sourdough starter already though and you want to add that to the bread for more tang, supplement 150 g/5 oz of the poolish in the flatbread recipe with your starter. Poolish is an active mixture that grows in size, so your container should be big enough to allow that to happen. If you choose to ignore this advice you may find yourself cleaning a stubborn mix of flour and water off the inside of your refrigerator.

There are no machines involved in the mixing of this dough. At Tartine Bakery, they use the expression 'turn' in reference to handling the dough, which moves away from the more aggressive idea of kneading. Chad described this approach to me as 'allowing the dough to accomplish much of the work passively', which altered my perspective on baking entirely. It's a good mindset to get yourself into. Gentle turning of the dough periodically, consideration of temperature, and time, are the three main factors at work here. This bread has a high hydration, designed to be baked as a flatbread. It's too wet to shape into a conventional loaf, but that's kind of the point.

The poolish should be made between 6–12 hours ahead of the dough, then allow yourself at least 3 hours to make the actual dough. You won't be physically working for those 3 hours, so a bottle of wine or a few beers does very well to pass the time. After you've mixed the dough, it needs a minimum of 6 hours in the refrigerator, to bulk ferment. Once that's done, it will need to be portioned then allowed to rest for a further 2–3 hours. What I'm getting at is that this is a rewarding but lengthy process. Give yourself plenty of time on each day for each process, especially the first time round. There is an old military saying called the Seven 'P's: Proper Prior Planning Prevents Piss Poor Performance. It's tacky, but sums up my sentiment perfectly.

BAM BASIC FLATBREAD DOUGH

The addition of smoked potatoes or Jerusalem artichokes (sunchokes) adds another dimension to the flatbread flavour, but it's by no means necessary. Also, if you are lactose intolerant or vegan then swap the milk in this recipe for water. The milk enriches the dough, but it's not essential. The potatoes can make the dough a little more difficult to pat out, but just don't go too thin. A good tip is to double the amount of poolish you make for the first time you try this, in case of any accidents, failures or spillages. It is imperative that you weigh out the ingredients for this recipe rather than using cup measures, which is why there are none below.

ESSENTIAL EQUIPMENT

small plastic container with lid for the poolish
large plastic container with a tight-fitting lid for
bulk rising the dough
weighing scales
dough scraper
cling film (plastic wrap)
8–10 x 450 g/1 lb containers with lids such as
disposable cups with lids/takeaway containers
tray for rolling dough

MAKES 8-9 BREADS

FOR THE POOLISH

10 g/¼ oz fresh yeast
100 g/3½ oz wholemeal (wholewheat) flour
100 g/3½ oz plain (all-purpose) flour

FOR THE DOUGH

375 g/13 oz plain (all-purpose) flour
190 g/6¾ oz strong white bread flour
190 g/6¾ oz strong wholemeal (wholewheat)
bread flour
7 g/1 teaspoon fresh yeast
23 g/¾ oz salt
350 g/12 oz Poolish (see above)
225 ml/8 fl oz whole (full-fat) milk
150 g/5 oz Smoked Potatoes or Jerusalem Artichokes
(optional; page 196)

1

First, make the poolish. The day before you make your dough mix 200 ml/7 fl oz cold water with the yeast in the small lidded container. Add the flours and use one hand to incorporate everything, making sure there are no pockets of dry flour or lumps of yeast. It should be thick and fairly smooth with a bit of effort, ending up with a mixture that resembles a thick milkshake.

2

Cover the poolish with the lid and mature in the refrigerator overnight, or for at least 6 hours. By this time the poolish should have doubled in size.

3

Now to make the dough. Weigh out the flours, yeast and salt into the large plastic container.

4

Reset the scales and weigh out the poolish.

5

Reset again, add the milk and 350 ml/12¼ fl oz water, and break down the poolish and the yeast with your hand. Give it all a good mix, then break the Smoked Potatoes over the top (if using). Now all you need to do is rest the mix with the lid securely on your tub for 30–40 minutes, or up to an hour if you're working in a cooler environment. This resting period is known as autolyse, which is the first step in the bulk fermentation. This is an important step and one that should always be observed. Autolyse allows the flour to absorb the liquid and encourages the gluten to bond into chains that will extend the elasticity of the dough, and ultimately improve the quality of the dough as well as the flavour.

6

Once everything has gotten to know each other, the next step is the first of three turns. To prevent the dough from sticking to your hands, wet one hand and forearm under warm water, slip your hand down the side of the tub, pinch a fistful of dough, gently lift the dough up and fold over to the opposite side of the container. Avoid hoisting the dough so high that it tears on the first turn; the dough is still weak at this stage and will have the least resistance of the three turns. Remember that aggression is not your friend here, and a gentle but firm approach will encourage growth and yield a better flavour. Repeat this move a further two times, pinching the areas of dough that haven't been turned already.

7

Place the lid back on the container, then leave in a warm place, undisturbed, for 30 minutes. Copy this method a second time, again leaving the dough covered and undisturbed for 30 minutes. As you progress through turns two and three you will find the dough more cooperative, and with each turn you should notice a higher elasticity in the dough and signs of activity happening. After the third turn, inspect your dough one final time before storing in the refrigerator overnight for bulk fermentation.

The dough you're looking at in the tub in front of you should be smooth, risen and slappable. If it's not you've fucked up somewhere along the line and sorry to say that attempting to rectify the dough at this stage is futile... but I bet you're happy you took my advice about making double the amount of poolish, right? Ensure the lid is fitted snugly to the tub when refrigerating, as any exposure to air will form a skin which will affect the rise.

—

8

After overnight bulk fermentation, the dough is ready to be portioned. It will be about 1.7 kg/3 lb 11 oz or 1.85 kg/4 lb 1 oz total weight (if using potato or artichoke). Take the lids off the small containers and get your scales ready along with a bowl of warm water for dipping your hand into when portioning. Remove the tub from the refrigerator. The dough should be billowy, stretchy and wet. This can get messy so always keep one hand free of dough for grabbing containers, texting, Instagram.... Dip one hand in the warm water, take a fistful of dough and weigh it out to 210 g/7½ oz.

Place the dough in the containers as you go, then secure the lids and leave in the refrigerator for a minimum of 2 hours. Portioning is quite traumatic for the dough, so the breads need this time to relax. If you attempt to pat out the dough too soon after portioning it'll be reluctant to cooperate. Now the dough is portioned it will retard at a very slow rate, held in a kind

of stasis. If you have a decent refrigerator the dough will be good for 2–3 days.

BARBECUE METHOD

Firing up a barbecue for a few breads may seem excessive, especially if you have a largish one. Take advantage and cook something to accompany the bread you're about to grill. I don't know how big your home barbecue is or what type of fuel you will be using so you need to rely on your own common sense to some degree and assess how to undertake this step yourself. I have a standard 50 cm (20 inch) barbecue that works perfectly, and out of sheer laziness and pyrotechnic tendencies I throw on a whole 5 kg/11 lb bag of charcoal. I do, however, avoid using kerosene fire lighters, as they can taint the flavour. Call me old fashioned, but a few strategically placed bits of newspaper and a match work for me.

These breads are a versatile string to have in your bow, especially if you don't have access to a pizza oven for the topped breads (pages 151–167) and are achievable in a backyard with most barbecues. Made a little ahead and with a bit of rest, they soften, making them perfect for wraps and will sop up the juices of whatever you decide to smuggle inside before stuffing it into your mouth.

ESSENTIAL EQUIPMENT

barbecue
tray for shaping dough
pizza peel
tongs
grill brush

MAKES 8–9 BREADS

1 x quantity BAM Basic Flatbread Dough (see left)
flour, for dusting

1

Light your barbecue in the usual fashion. Wait for the flames to die down and the coals to glow. This is the perfect opportunity to set up the work surface and gather the equipment. I also like to make sure

that everything I need is within grabbing distance of where I'm cooking so I'm not frantically beating a path across the garden searching for a pair of tongs to flip burning bread with. When the barbecue has settled, rake the coals over to one side. When you're happy with the coals, pop the grill over and retrieve the first bread from the refrigerator.

—

2

Next, take a handful of flour and put it in the middle of the tray. 'Bread Dust', as it's affectionately known at BAM, has a tendency to get everywhere, so if you're wearing your best frock or three-piece suit, stick an apron on. Using one of your hands, scoop the dough out of the container onto a tray, keeping the dough as close to a ball shape as possible. The idea is to keep the dough in a uniform bun shape so when you pat it out it stays round. Toss a little more flour on top – it's better to have more flour than less as any excess flour can be brushed off before cooking. Start patting out the dough by applying a little pressure with your fingertips, gently working the bread into a saucer-sized round, about 1 cm/½ inch thick. Gently brush off the excess flour, pick the bread up and place the dough close to the lip of the pizza peel.

→

—
3

Give the peel the tiniest of shakes to make sure the dough isn't stuck then with a quick flick of the wrist transfer the dough from the peel onto a medium heat on the grill. Drop the dough on a very hot part of the grill and it'll char too quickly and has a tendency stick. A nice medium heat will cook the bread through, colour the base nicely and give you the desired rise.

—
4

You're looking for a little range of bumps to form on top. Keep an eye on the base, making sure it's not burning.

—
5

Ease the tongs underneath and have a peek at the underside, if the colour is good with a decent char but not burning and it comes off the grill with little or no resistance then persuade the dough off the grill and flip the bread onto a slightly hotter area of the grill. The bread should be more or less cooked at this point – the idea is to get a decent char on those bubbles that formed on top. The high heat also prevents the bread from drying out too much. This char will give you texture as well as flavour.

—
6

Scrape the grill clean and repeat with the rest of the dough. As you grow in confidence and can recognize how the dough behaves you may want to start cooking a few breads at a time. Obviously the breads are best served immediately, but if you're not serving straight away, keep the breads loosely covered with a clean dish towel and flash over the grill when needed. Try your bread. Pull it apart, smell it, then take a bite. If it's stodgy inside there is a good chance it's undercooked. This is a process you have to learn, and like me you'll probably fail the first few times while you're working things out. Slathering the breads in melted salted butter is always a good move. This is also when Marmite in a squeeze bottle really comes into its own.

PIZZA OVEN METHOD

Your eyes are one of the most important tools you possess when cooking. We have all had good pizzas and flatbreads (I hope) and bad ones (I hope too, each has its place in my life). However the shitty frozen pizza baked anaemic dry for convenience in your kitchen oven at home is the opposite to what we are looking to achieve. The bad pizza is a good visual to have when you're first getting to grips with the whole business of cooking this type of flatbread. The bread should start to react fairly quickly if the oven is at a good temperature.

ESSENTIAL EQUIPMENT

oven brush
tray for shaping dough
2 pizza peels (one for loading and one for retrieving)

MAKES 8-9 BREADS

flour, for dusting
1 x quantity **BAM** Basic Flatbread Dough (page 58)

1

When the time comes to cook, fire up the oven with an end goal of **250–300°C/480–570°F.** While the oven is coming up to temperature, get all your other ingredients and equipment ready. The dough will become unworkable and stick like shit to a blanket if you don't add your toppings (pages 151–167) and get them in the oven quickly. Once it's reached full temperature, push the coals to one side and brush the oven floor.

—
2

Heap a generous handful of flour on the tray, then, using one hand, place the first piece of dough on top of the flour pile. Pinch any ragged edges up to the top of the dough to create a uniform bun shape with the same hand; you'll notice that little bits of dough stick to your fingers, so it helps to keep the other hand clean for grabbing what you need to top the bread.

—
3

Flour the top of the dough and gently push down into the middle with your fingertips 3-4 times, working your way towards the edge of the dough. Flip and repeat this move until you end up with a round of dough **25.5-26.5 cm (10-10½ inches)** in diameter. Try and get the dough as flat and even as possible, to a thickness of around 1 cm (½ inch); the most important thing to avoid is tearing the dough or patting it too thinly. If you tear the bread, try and pull the surrounding dough over the hole, but if you can't fix it, don't bother topping the bread.

Cook the bread without any topping rather than waste it... perfectly good for dipping in olive oil.

—
4

When the dough is shaped, lift it off the tray onto the back of your hand and lightly tap off a bit of the excess flour. Flip it onto the peel and reshape back into a round. Don't drop the ball now. Check there aren't any edges stuck to the peel, and if there are, dust them with a touch of flour and ease a knife or dough scraper under the dough, giving the peel the tiniest of shakes back and forth until the dough moves freely.

—
5

Add any toppings to the bread. If you're making the Lamb Offal Flatbread (page 160), now is the time to pipe on the meat mixture and spread it over the dough.

—
6

Load the bread into the oven. Try to gauge your heat with the first bread. I would avoid placing the bread too close to the flames if you have the space. If the oven is too hot the bread will burn, won't cook and will be impossible to turn or move. Only when the bread has formed a light crust on the bottom after a minute or two can you attempt to move it.

—
7

The breads cook for about 6 minutes in the restaurant in an oven that runs on gas and holds a consistent temperature. The time your bread will take to cook will depend on certain variables. The size and heat of your oven and how thick or flat you decided to pat the dough out to are all key factors. I like a full spectrum of colour on my flatbreads ranging from dark to light, this enhances texture and flavour. There is a difference between dark and burnt though. As the flatbread is approaching your desired colour you will need to rotate the bread 180 degrees and colour the other side. Slot the edge of the second peel, or what I call a retriever

peel, under the bread, lift it ever so slightly and coax it round half a turn. Once cooked evenly, remove from the oven with the pizza peel. Finish your bread with whichever extra toppings are required before eating, see page 160 for the Lamb Offal Flatbread.

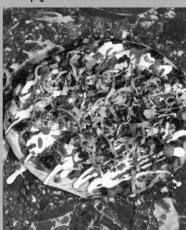

DOMESTIC OVEN METHOD

This is an alternative method for cooking flatbreads if you don't have a pizza oven. It's important to note that this method will not provide you with the same results you will achieve in a pizza oven but I am well pleased with the experimental runs I did at home, and wanted to include this method because quite obviously not everyone has access to a pizza oven. I tested this in my oven which is a pretty standard electric Miele. It's safe to say if your oven is a complete piece of shit, your bread might not turn out well, though saying that the Squid Ink Flatbread (page 154) is pretty achievable in most ovens because you're just baking it; for this flatbread, you'll need to have the pan 12 cm (4½ in) from the grill, otherwise you'll incinerate the egg.

ESSENTIAL EQUIPMENT

---

well-seasoned cast-iron pan or pizza stone
2 pizza peels (one for loading and one for retrieving)

MAKES 8-10

---

1 x quantity **BAM** Basic Flatbread Dough (page 58)
flour, for dusting

1

Preheat the grill (broiler) as high as it will go, then place a well-seasoned cast iron pan (this won't work as well with a brand new pan) or pizza stone 7-10 cm (3 in) from the grill. Leave to heat up for at least 15 minutes.

—

2

While the grill is heating, take your portioned dough and place it on a well-floured plate. Pinch up the dough to make a uniform bun shape, as on page 59.

—

3

Next, pat out the dough. Follow the method on page 59 – if making the Squid Ink Flatbread, only pat out to 2.5 cm (1 inch) thick/12.75 cm (5 inches) in diameter.

—

4

Flip the dough onto the back of your hand, tap lightly to remove excess flour, and transfer to the pizza peel.

—

5

If you're making the Squid Ink Flatbread (page 154), brush the top of the dough with melted butter. For other flatbreads, now is the time to add any toppings.

—

6

Working quickly, open the oven door and slide the dough off the pizza peel into the pan or onto the stone and then shut the door and cook until crisp, browned and with the odd scorch mark. Time will very much depend on your oven, but roughly 6 minutes.

—

7

If you're making the Squid Ink Flatbread (page 154), use a teaspoon to make a small dent in the centre of the bread. Drop an egg yolk into each dent, then drip some melted butter over the yolk and return to the oven to warm the yolk through. Finish with the cod's roe.

FLAVOUR
TEXTURE
EXECUTION
PRESENTATION

Because I started cooking so late in life, I felt like I had to fill the chasm of knowledge and experience that I lacked by mentally recording and analysing everything I consumed. The nose-to-tail discipline of St. JOHN was the best tutelage I could have wished for. I also had the privilege of travelling a fair bit with Trevor and Fergus, which further enhanced my education. These things combined have defined how I now approach food.

As a result, I've subconsciously coached my brain to explore and evaluate ways in which I could manipulate or improve (if possible) whatever I'm tasting at that moment. I see any opportunity to eat as an opportunity to learn, as well as to have a good time. But I do miss dining with an absence of analysis – sometimes, I wish I could sit down and eat a meal the way I used to. That said, I'm very aware that this process is a necessary tool for any culinary creativity that I might possess. Maybe that's why I have a mild fixation on the food of my youth, and why the dishes at **BAM** are always punctuated with nostalgia.

When it comes to writing recipes, I value flavour above all else, and the rest just works around that. I hear myself saying 'I can taste it in my mind' when I'm trying to explain new ideas to my wife Kate; dishes and flavours that I haven't had time to develop niggle me, and a tiny part of my brain is working around the clock to connect the dots to bring them to fruition. But, once I have the flavour nailed, I work backwards from that, usually in this order:

FLAVOUR
TEXTURE
EXECUTION
PRESENTATION

David Chang once said that life is too short to be mediocre. I've burned this mantra into my psyche, and it's ever-present when I'm developing a recipe or making decisions about the restaurant. I believe all of the recipes within the covers of this book, however diverse, have this as a common thread. It's easy to be generic, because it requires less effort, but that's not what I wanted this book to be about.

I've found turning what appears on the plate at **BAM** into recipes a challenging but ultimately rewarding process, and I know that when people are reading these words, I'm going to feel like the Wizard of Oz did when Toto pulled back the green silk curtain, exposing him for the vulnerable old man he actually was:

'Oh no my dear, I'm a very good man, I'm just a very bad chef.'
'But what about the heart recipe you promised to Tin Man?'

When Kate and I started **BAM** it was about having fun. I decided to write this book because I wanted others to have fun with these recipes too – that's the point, right? Eating and drinking is and always will be the most joyful of pursuits, and I find both deeply satisfying.

I've gone into as much detail as I possibly can in regards to equipment, preparation, execution and inevitable variables in an attempt to make these recipes approachable, and so that the cooking part stands a good chance of being fun.

BRUNCH

VIETNAMESE SCRAMBLED EGGS WITH SESAME BREAD

This is a dish we used to serve as staff meal at St. **JOHN** Bread and **Wine** from time to time. I'm not sure why we called it Vietnamese Scrambled Eggs, but it's basically scrambled eggs with Asian flavours, and it's fucking tasty. If you can't be bothered to make the Sesame Bread by all means use whatever bread you have at home, but preferably something with a bit of texture, like sourdough. Sweet coffee goes well with this. Or even a White Russian.

ESSENTIAL EQUIPMENT
non-stick frying pan (skillet)
rubber spatula

SERVES 4
3–4 cloves garlic, thinly sliced
2 thumb-sized pieces of ginger, peeled
and finely chopped
sunflower or vegetable oil, for frying
2 red chillies, finely chopped
3 spring onions (scallions), whites thinly sliced,
greens reserved
1 bunch coriander (cilantro), stems sliced, leaves left
whole and reserved
25 g (1 oz/2 tablespoons) butter
8 eggs, beaten
fish sauce, to taste
salt

FOR THE SALAD
400 g/14 oz bean sprouts
reserved greens of the spring onions (see above),
finely sliced
2 tablespoons Pickled Red Chillies (page 201)
2 tablespoons Pickled Red Onions (page 200)
1 tablespoon olive oil
juice of ½–1 lime
reserved coriander leaves (see above)

TO SERVE
4 **BAM** Flatbreads (pages 56–63), topped with sesame
seeds and a dash of sesame oil after cooking
8 rashers **BAM** Bacon, or shop bought, grilled
(page 50; optional)
dried baby shrimp (optional)
2 tablespoons shop-bought crispy fried onions

In a non-stick frying pan (skillet) over a low heat, soften the garlic and ginger in a little oil for 2 minutes. Add the chillies with a pinch of salt and cook for a further minute. Add the whites of the spring onions (scallions) and the coriander (cilantro) stalks and cook for 1–2 minutes more. Don't cook the latter for too long as they will lose their vibrant green colour. Remove from the heat and set aside.

Next, toss all the salad ingredients in a mixing bowl until well combined, and set aside.

Wipe the non-stick frying pan clean, and then get the pan hot over a high heat. Melt the butter in the pan and add the garlic, ginger and chilli mix. When it starts to sizzle, add the eggs and stir with a rubber spatula. Turn the heat down to low. Keep stirring and turning the eggs, then add a good splash of fish sauce, bearing in mind that this is all the seasoning the eggs are going to get. I like to go pretty heavy with it – at least ½ tablespoon – but really it depends how salty and funky you want it. I'd recommend tasting a little of the egg once it's mixed in to check. Continue to cook the eggs for around 2 minutes – you want them just cooked and super silky, as opposed to dried out and rubbery.

Place the breads on plates. Distribute the scrambled eggs onto each bread and top with the salad. Add the bacon and dried baby shrimp (if using) and the crispy fried onions. Serve with steak knives for ease of eating.

CRISPY PANCAKES

You have to come from a certain place in time to be into Findus Crispy Pancakes. According to my research, you can only buy them in the UK, Ireland and Italy (the Italian brand is called Sofficini and they have flavours I've never tried before, like Tomato and Mozzarella), and the most readily available filling I can find here is Beef and Onion, priced at four pancakes for £1 ($1.30). I tested this recipe with a variety of fillings (see suggestions below), and the younger chefs at **BAM** thought they tasted great, but had never eaten the original. Findus describe them as coming in a variety of savoury flavours, each oozing with tasty fillings and coated in delicious crispy breadcrumbs. I don't know about you, but that description gets my juices going. I'm particularly attracted to the word 'crispy' – throw 'oozing with tasty fillings' into the same sentence and I'm cashing in all my chips. When I tried one recently though, I have to say a small part of me, the part that loved these as a kid, died of disappointment. Surprise, surprise, they aren't as great as I remembered. Then again, I loved watching the film *Teen Wolf* as a kid, and that hasn't aged well either. Not like the *Back to the Future* trilogy...though realistically you'd still watch *Teen Wolf* if there was nothing else on the telly. In both cases, I won't let a stark modern-day truth warp my romantic, nostalgic childhood memory, one that I'm sure I share with hundreds, if not thousands, of you. These pancakes are also a fun and easy way to use leftovers; I've tried leftover curry takeaway with lime pickle, Mapo Tofu (page 76), bolognese with a dash of Tabasco, lasagne, shepherd's pie, St. JOHN Rarebit mix (page 159), ratatouille (drained of liquid) with mozzarella or fish pie mix. If you're looking for a dessert to follow these, I would suggest staying on the same nostalgia trip and serving butterscotch flavour Angel Delight.

ESSENTIAL EQUIPMENT
25 cm (10 inch) non-stick frying pan (skillet)

SERVES 6

FOR THE PANCAKES
1 whole egg, plus 1 yolk
280 ml (9½ fl oz/1¼ cups) whole (full-fat) milk
pinch of caster (superfine) sugar
pinch of salt
2 tablespoons butter, melted
110 g (4 oz/scant 1 cup) plain (all-purpose) flour
neutral oil, such as sunflower, for frying
sea salt flakes, to serve
pickles of your choice, to serve

FOR THE FILLING
400 g/14 oz bacon lardons
2 tablespoons truffle honey
250 g/9 oz Ogleshield, Comte or mature
Cheddar cheese, grated
1 egg, beaten
freshly ground black pepper

FOR THE CRUMB COATING
4 eggs
2 tablespoons Dijon mustard
50 g (2 oz/scant ½ cup) plain (all-purpose) flour
100 g (3½ oz/2 cups) panko breadcrumbs

First, make the pancakes. Whisk the egg and yolk with the milk, sugar and salt in a small jug. Add the melted butter, then pour the milk and egg mixture a little at a time into the flour in a mixing bowl, whisking vigorously to disperse any lumps. Chill in the refrigerator for 30–45 minutes.

To cook the pancakes, heat a 25 cm (10 inch) non-stick or well-seasoned frying pan (skillet) over a medium heat. Pour in a teaspoon of oil to coat the base of the pan then tip 60 ml (2 fl oz/¼ cup) pancake batter into the middle of the pan, moving the mix around the base of the pan until it is completely coated. It's important not to have any holes in the pancakes for the filling to escape through, so if you spot any, fill them with a few drops of pancake mix. If your pan is bigger or smaller, that's fine – as long as your pancakes are thin, you will be able to fill them. Once all the pancakes are cooked, stack on a chopping (cutting) board and allow to cool completely.

In a small frying pan over a medium heat, fry the bacon lardons until crisp and cooked, around 5–8 minutes. Toss in the truffle honey, stir to combine, then allow to cool.

To assemble the pancakes, spoon the bacon onto one half of each pancake, leaving about 1.5 cm (¾ inch) space from the edge. Distribute the cheese and give each one a generous grind of black pepper. Paint the borders of every pancake with the beaten egg, pushing any rogue bits of cheese or bacon

away from the edge, as it will impede the sealing process. Fold the bare half over so the eggy edges meet and seal the pancake. Allow to chill in the refrigerator to firm up for about 1 hour if you can spare the time, but if not, just take extra care when crumbing.

To crumb the pancakes, whisk the eggs and mustard together in a wide, shallow bowl, then tip the flour into a separate wide, shallow bowl and spread the breadcrumbs across a baking sheet. Give each pancake a light coating of flour, shaking off any excess. Now, dunk each pancake in the egg and mustard mix, lift out and place on the baking sheet with the breadcrumbs and toss around until coated. You can now refrigerate or cook immediately.

I use the same frying pan to cook the crispy pancakes as I do the pancake batter, which means I can fit two in the pan at a time, and it's a manageable number to cook nicely. I have some paper towels by the hob (stove) to clean the pan out after each round. The breadcrumbs soak up a fair bit of oil, and they will scorch if there isn't enough, so keep adding a little to the pan after each batch. Shallow fry the pancakes over a medium heat until golden on one side, around 3 minutes, then flip and repeat on the other side. Drain on paper towels, then keep warm in a low oven while you cook the rest. Sprinkle with sea salt flakes and serve immediately with your choice of pickles.

BAM REUBEN

I have a weakness for corned beef, pastrami, salt beef, ox tongue, boiled brisket... anything that can be consumed with mustard, pickles and bread. The pinker the better, hot, salty, fatty, I'll take it any way it comes. Schwartz Deli's extra fatty smoked meat sandwich is something I go out of my way to eat when I'm in Montreal; it's second only to my beloved salt beef bagel, double pickle, double mustard, from Beigel Bake in Brick Lane, London. I've taken some of my favourite elements from each of these sandwiches and combined them into what we bill as the 'BAM Reuben'. It arrives at your table complete with pickles on the side and either crisps (potato chips if you're from the USA or Canada) or shoestring fries. When I went on a school trip to Le Touquet, France, as a kid, it blew my mind that they served ham and cheese baguettes in baskets with ready salted crisps on the side. On the fucking SIDE! Not as a treat after your main sandwich. This shouldn't still excite me to the extent that it does, but that's why I serve sandwiches like this today. Purists might argue that the sandwich we make at BAM doesn't qualify as a classic Reuben because we use ox tongue, it isn't served with Russian dressing, and it doesn't come in rye bread – so yes, come to think of it, it's very much a bastardized version, but we've gotten away with it for this long so I'm not going to go changing it now... plus, it's our most popular item on the brunch menu. We build the sandwich then melt St. JOHN Rarebit (page 159) into it by toasting it in our wood-fired oven, but don't worry, that's easily achieved in a domestic oven.

I love that this type of sandwich is composed almost entirely with preserved food designed to have long or extended shelf lives. Pickled cucumber, sauerkraut, mustard, salted meat and cheese. Every ingredient goes through a process before being united between bread. Technically you can buy all the accoutrements for this from the supermarket. No one is judging you, least of all me.

This requires space in a refrigerator for at least seven days, so planning and commitment are both essential if you embark on this recipe. If, however, that's not possible, you can enquire about brined (pickled) tongue at your local butcher.

ESSENTIAL EQUIPMENT
airtight container large enough to fit an ox tongue
and the brine
butcher's needle or metal skewer

SERVES 4-6

FOR THE BRINE
2 star anise
1 tablespoon coriander seeds
1 tablespoon caraway seeds
2 bay leaves
250 g (9 oz/1 cup plus 2 tablespoons) fine sea salt
250 g (9 oz/1 cup plus 2 tablespoons) light brown
or demerara sugar
2 tablespoons saltpeter (potassium nitrate; optional)

FOR THE TONGUE
1 ox tongue or 2 veal tongues, stabbed multiple times
with a butcher's needle or metal skewer
2 bay leaves
1 tablespoon black peppercorns
1 tablespoon cloves

FOR THE SANDWICH
4-6 BAM Flatbreads (pages 56-63; I like to jazz
this up a bit by adding 1 tablespoon caraway seeds
during the first stage of the dough method) or 8-12 slices
good quality sourdough
300 g/11 oz St. JOHN Rarebit mix (page 159)
Sauerkraut (page 201)
French's Mustard
Dill Pickles (page 200)
Crisps (potato chips), to serve

📷 PP74/75

To make the brine, in a large saucepan bring 1 litre (34 fl oz/ 4¼ cups) water to a simmer with the star anise, coriander seeds, caraway seeds and bay leaves for 10–15 minutes. Dissolve the salt, sugar and saltpeter (if using) in the water and allow to cool completely before refrigerating. If possible, refrigerate the brine in the container you intend to brine the tongue in so you know you have enough space to store the meat with roughly a 3 cm (1¼ inch) covering of brine. A deep plastic container with a tight fitting lid is ideal. Once thoroughly chilled, place the tongue in the container and weigh down with a plate, keeping the tongue completely submerged. Replace the lid and refrigerate for 7–10 days. The length of time needed will depend on the size of the tongue – it should feel firm.

When ready to cook, place the tongue in a lidded saucepan of cold water and bring to the boil. Once boiled, drain and refresh the water, adding the bay leaves, peppercorns and cloves. Bring the water to a boil again. Reduce to a simmer and weigh the tongue down with a plate. Cover and simmer for 2½–3 hours, checking the tongue after this time by poking it with a metal skewer or thin knife. If the skewer goes in and comes out with little or no resistance, the tongue is ready. If not, continue to cook, checking frequently until it is done. Allow the tongue to cool in the cooking liquid until you can handle it comfortably.

Once cool, you'll need to peel the tongue. Remove from the cooking liquid and place on a chopping (cutting) board, keeping the liquid to one side. If it's too cool though, it can become quite difficult. The outer skin you need to remove is quite obvious. Work your finger under the skin from the back – it should peel away with ease. You may have to use a paring knife to scrape the thinner skin on the underside of the tongue near the tip – I've noticed that this can be a little reluctant to come away, regardless of how well I've cooked the tongue, so don't worry if this is the case. Once fully peeled, return it to the cooking liquid to cool completely. Store in the refrigerator until required.

When ready to serve, remove the tongue from the refrigerator and place on a chopping board. Cut the tongue in half so that the thicker end is separated from the thinner end. Cut the thicker end widthways into 5 mm (¼ inch) slices, then cut the thinner end lengthways into 5 mm (¼ inch) slices also. Once sliced, tip the tongue back into the cooking liquid and warm through over a low–medium heat. This can sit quite comfortably while you are bringing the other ingredients together.

Preheat the oven to 180°C/350°F/Gas Mark 4.

To assemble, have your BAM Flatbreads or sourdough grilled and ready. Shake the slices of tongue to get rid of any excess water, then place 6–8 slices on one side of the flatbreads, or if using sourdough, on half of the slices of bread. Top the ox tongue with 2 tablespoons of St. JOHN Rarebit mix, followed by the Sauerkraut and a squeeze of mustard. Fold the other half of the flatbread over, or if using sourdough, top each with a slice of bread. Secure with toothpicks, and bake until the cheese is melted, around 6 minutes.

Put on plates and serve immediately with Dill Pickles and crisps (potato chips) on the side.

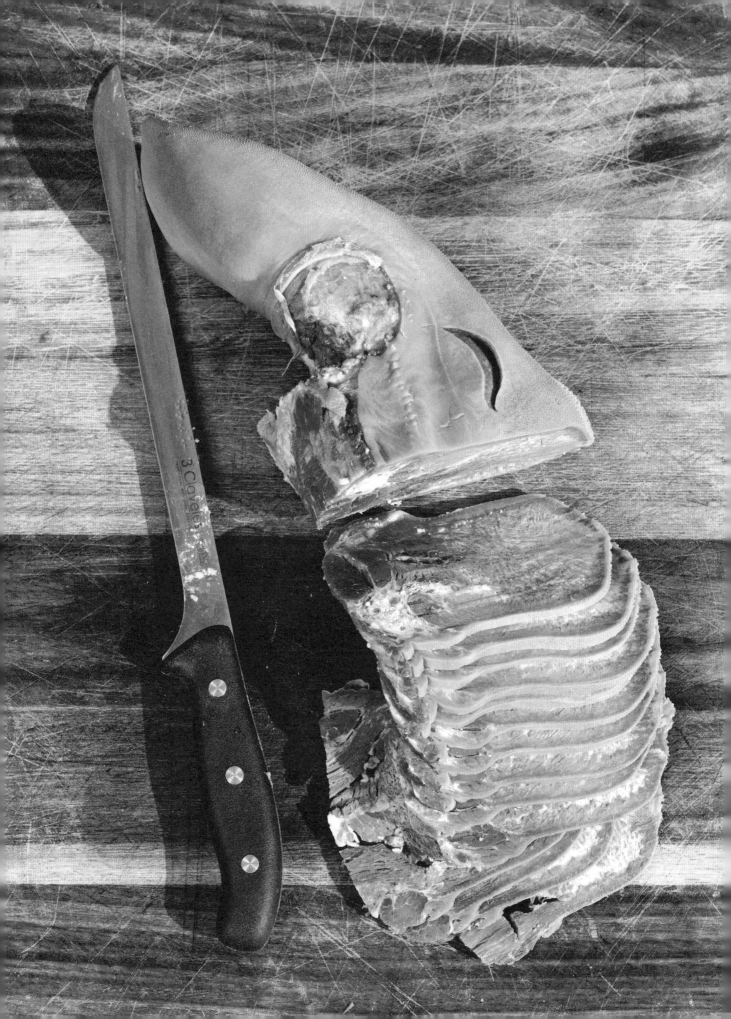

MAPO TOFU, HASH BROWNS AND FRIED EGGS

The best version I had of mapo tofu was at Mission Chinese on Orchard street in NYC; Danny Bowien took this classic Chinese dish and amplified every flavour, much like my approach to reworking *lahmacun* for our Lamb Offal Flatbread (page 160). This is an adaptation of his recipe, revised with ingredients that are easy to track down in decent Asian supermarkets or online in the UK (I use the Lao Gan Ma brand; there's more information in the glossary on page 204). Given the choice, I'd always eat something spicy for breakfast, and mapo and hash browns is a winning combination. This is my death row meal.

ESSENTIAL EQUIPMENT
2 x 900 g (2 lb) loaf pans
tin cans for weighing down the potato
hand-held (immersion) blender or food processor
deep-fat fryer

SERVES 4-6

FOR THE HASH BROWNS
500 g/1 lb 2 oz Yukon Gold or Maris Piper potatoes,
peeled and grated
½ teaspoon salt
vegetable oil, for frying

FOR THE MAPO TOFU
90 g/3¼ oz dried mushrooms, ideally a mix of porcini
and shiitake
8 cloves garlic, minced
25 g/1 oz green Szechuan peppercorns,
toasted and ground
1 tablespoon dried chilli flakes
3 tablespoons vegetable oil
2 tablespoons tomato purée (paste)
2 tablespoons spicy Chinese hot chilli bean paste
(also known as spicy broad bean paste)
150 g/5 oz kohlrabi, peanuts and tofu in chilli oil
150 g/5 oz preserved black beans in chilli oil
330 ml (11 fl oz/generous 1¼ cups) India pale ale (IPA)
1 tablespoon Szechuan peppercorn (prickly) oil
350 g/12⅓ oz firm tofu, diced

TO SERVE
4-6 duck eggs
vegetable oil, for frying
4 teaspoons truffle oil
100g/3½ oz enoki mushrooms, trimmed and separated
2 tablespoons Pickled Shimeji Mushrooms
(page 201; optional)
4 teaspoons Mission Spice (page 197)
2 tablespoons shop-bought crispy fried onions
1 teaspoon dried chilli flakes
small handful coriander (cilantro), washed and dried

First, make the hash browns. Preheat the oven to 150°C/300°F/Gas Mark 2.

In a colander over the sink, rinse the grated potatoes until the water is virtually clear. Squeeze dry and add the salt.

Line one of the loaf pans with baking (parchment) paper. Add the potato to the lined tin. Place another rectangle of baking paper over the top of the potato. Put the second loaf pan, base-side down, on top of the potato, cover with a tight layer of aluminium foil and bake for 1½–2 hours. Try eating a pinch – if it's soft it's ready, but if it's a bit raw still, recover the pan and cook for a little longer, until done.

Allow the potato to cool slightly, then remove the aluminium foil and press the living daylights out of it with the second pan still on top using something heavy, such as a couple of tin cans. Find a spot in your refrigerator to accommodate the loaf pans and the weight. I've used a brick and a paving slab in the past, but I'm reluctant to recommend you doing this as I don't want to be responsible for any damages and your partner asking why you've got a filthy paving stone in the refrigerator. Chill for a minimum of 4 hours, until completely cold.

Once chilled, transfer the hash from the loaf pan onto a chopping (cutting) board, removing the paper as you do. Cut in half widthways with a sharp serrated knife, then cut each half in half again. Cut each quarter diagonally in half, giving you 8 triangles in total. Return to the refrigerator while you prepare the tofu.

Place the dried mushrooms in a small bowl and cover with 500 ml (16 fl oz/2 cups) boiling water. Allow to soak for 15–20 minutes. Blitz the mushrooms with their soaking water to a rough paste with a hand-held (immersion) blender or food processor.

In a large frying pan (skillet) over a low–medium heat, fry the garlic, ground Szechuan peppercorns and dried chilli in the oil for 1 minute, until fragrant, making sure the garlic doesn't catch and burn. Add the tomato purée and bean paste. Cook for 3–5 minutes, then add the mushroom paste and kohlrabi and black beans. Mix to combine, pour in the IPA and simmer for 10 minutes. Remove from the heat and drizzle with the Szechuan peppercorn (prickly) oil. At this point, you can add the tofu and eat straight away, or pour into an airtight container and store in the refrigerator for up to a week. If eating straight away, put the mapo pan back on a low heat to keep warm while you make the rest of the dish.

Heat a deep-fat fryer with the vegetable oil to 190°C/375°F, or as high as your fryer will go. Remove the hash browns from the refrigerator and cook until crisp and golden brown, approximately 5–6 minutes.

While the hash browns are cooking, fry the duck eggs in a little oil in a frying pan over medium heat.

Add the diced tofu to the mapo and gently stir until coated and warmed through.

To serve, place the hash browns onto a large serving platter, then top with the tofu, eggs, truffle oil, enoki and pickled mushrooms, Mission Spice, crispy fried onions, chilli flakes and coriander (cilantro).

LEFTOVER PIZZA FRENCH TOAST

I first made this topped with mapo tofu at **BAM** for staff brunch. Nowhere does mapo pizza in London... yet. If you want to make a mapo pizza, use the **Mapo Tofu** recipe on page **76** for the base sauce, then switch out the tofu for large chunks of mozzarella and follow the **BAM** Flatbread recipe on pages **56-63**. Domino's **New Yorker, American Hot or Meateor™** are my personal favourites for this recipe, but saying that, Domino's is the only pizza I can get delivered to my house, so that's probably why. I get genuine pleasure from cold pizza. The pure shittiness of a chain takeaway pizza lends itself perfectly to this dish, however, I experimented with a Yard Sale (an excellent sourdough pizza place in London) Holy Pepperoni pizza, which produced equally fine results, proving that legit pizza can hold its own here, too. Scale this up or down, depending on your leftovers. I believe Leftover Pizza French Toast has mystical hangover-curing properties.

ESSENTIAL EQUIPMENT
wide, shallow bowl, big enough to fit a pizza slice
non-stick or well-seasoned frying pan (skillet)

SERVES 2-4
3 egg yolks
6-7 leftover pizza slices, chilled
butter, for frying
salt and freshly ground black pepper

TO SERVE (OPTIONAL)
BAM Bacon (page 50) or shop-bought bacon,
grilled until crisp
pork sausages, grilled
Smoked Pig's Cheeks (page 53), sliced
and fried until crisp
Comté, Ogleshield or Emmental cheese, grated
Marmite
ketchup
hot sauce or sriracha sauce
maple syrup
truffle honey

Preheat the oven to 110°C/225°F/Gas Mark ¼. Beat the egg yolks in a shallow bowl or dish that's big enough to accommodate a pizza slice. Place the pizza slice in the egg for 2–3 minutes, turning a couple of times until well coated. Repeat with the rest of the slices.

Place a non-stick or well-seasoned frying pan (skillet) over a medium heat, add a knob of butter, wait for the butter to froth then add the pizza slices crust-side down. Season the topped side with a pinch of salt and a grind of pepper. When the crust side is golden, flip and fry the topped side. Drain on paper towels, then keep warm in the oven while you fry the rest of the slices.

To serve, pile onto a large platter, along with any of the suggested sides and condiments.

CINNAMON AND BANANA FLATBREAD

I'm pretty sure this is the only dish that made it through our first few brunch menus. We created a menu of things we thought people would like eating or absolutely must have at brunch – it was delicious, but 'vanilla', and so different to what we were serving at dinner. It kind of felt like having a bath with your socks on. We went to great lengths curing salmon, making cream cheese, poaching eggs to go on avocado... and hit rock bottom with the most inspiring of dishes: berries with granola, yogurt and honey. It took a while, but we finally found our voice with brunch, and believe we now offer one of the most exciting, alternative breakfast menus in London.

Bananas are great mashed up and spread over grilled flatbread with honey and cinnamon and a little sesame, but to get close to what we do at the restaurant, you'll need access to a pizza oven, or use a pizza stone in a very hot oven (page 60). Follow the basic dough recipe on page 58, omitting the Smoked Potatoes, unless you're some sort of freak that likes smoked potato and banana as a taste combination. However, don't feel you have to limit yourself in terms of experimentation of the right kind – raspberries or blackberries, poached peaches and whipped cream all work brilliantly.

ESSENTIAL EQUIPMENT
pizza oven, pizza stone or cast-iron frying pan (skillet)
(pages 60–62)
2 pizza peels

SERVES 4
½ quantity **BAM** Basic Flatbread Dough (page 58)
50 g (3½ oz/½ stick) butter, melted
6–8 large bananas, sliced
demerara sugar, for sprinkling
ground cinnamon, for sprinkling
250 ml (8 fl oz/generous 1 cup) crème fraîche
Nutella, to serve (optional)

Make the dough in exactly the same way and as described on page 58, dividing it into four. Shape a piece into a round and transfer to a pizza peel. Using a pastry brush, paint the entire surface of the bread with melted butter, taking care not to splash any on the peel as this can cause the dough to stick, which for this particular bread will be a disaster.

Place ¼ of the sliced banana onto the dough, with about 3 cm (1¼ inch) between each piece. Sprinkle the bread liberally with sugar, then check the bread isn't stuck to the peel by giving it a gentle shake and load the bread into the oven (see pages 60 and 62 for methods) a little further away from the flame than you would for a savoury flatbread, the reason being that the sugar needs a chance to melt before caramelizing. Give the bread a turn with your retrieving peel. These flatbreads require the most vigilance; the sugar will taste at its best when it turns a deep amber, but this technique of cooking makes it almost impossible to attain a perfectly uniform caramelization over the entire bread, and inevitably there will be one or two dark, bitter spots that will actually add complexity to the end flavour of the bread. Watch as the sugar gets darker and starts to bubble and keep turning accordingly. Pull the bread out and inspect it if need be, but cook the bread until it's as dark as you dare to go, around 5–6 minutes.

Pull the bread from the oven. Sounds obvious but caramelized sugar gets very hot and takes a while to cool, so watch your fingers. As the sugar cools it'll start to harden into a glaze, giving the crust a fine crunch. Repeat with the remaining dough to make four flatbreads.

Finish with a few shakes of cinnamon and a blob of crème fraîche. A pro would dip the crusts into Nutella.

SNACKS

BORSCHTBACK

At BAM, this is on the snack menu. Shop-bought beetroot (beet) juice takes the pain and mess out of peeling and juicing your own. There aren't many alternatives to horseradish juice, so you do ideally need access to a juicer to make this. However, you can extract some juice from jars of freshly grated horseradish at a push.

ESSENTIAL EQUIPMENT
juicer
cocktail sticks
shot glasses

MAKES 1.25 LITRES (42 FL OZ/5 CUPS)
1 litre (34 fl oz/4¼ cups) beetroot (beet) juice
180 ml (6 fl oz/¾ cup) pickled walnut vinegar
50 ml (1¾ fl oz/¼ cup) horseradish juice

TO SERVE
ice-cold vodka
pickled walnuts, quartered
smoked eel, chopped into bite-sized pieces

Mix the beetroot (beet) juice, pickled walnut vinegar and horseradish juice together in a jug (pitcher). Stir with a spoon, funnel into a screw cap bottle and chill until needed.

Pour a measure of vodka into a shot glass, followed by a measure of the beetroot mix into a separate shot glass. Pop a quarter of pickled walnut onto a cocktail stick, followed by a piece of smoked eel. Shoot the vodka, shoot the borschtback, and then eat the pickled walnut and eel.

This is also great served with oysters, preferably shucked by someone else.

CAVIAR AND SOUR CREAM AND CHIVE CRISPS

Perfect finger food if you are hosting an orgy.

SERVES SEVERAL
can of caviar, as large as you can afford
1 x tube Sour Cream and Chive Pringles

📷 **P86/87**

Pretty simple. Open your big ass can of caviar, pop the Pringles and use to scoop out.

CENTURY EGG WITH ANCHOVY DRESSING AND CRISPY PIG'S SKIN

Have you ever eaten a century egg? There is a saying 'the first bite is with the eye'. Let's just say that putting something that looks akin to Fungus the Bogeyman's dissected scrotum into your mouth is pretty intimidating. I was fascinated and appalled in equal measure when I first saw one in a restaurant in London's Chinatown. 'There is no way that can be good to eat,' I remember thinking, and politely declined the offer to partake. I was intrigued though, and watched as the other diners at the table tucked into them with gusto. It was years later when I ate my first century egg. It was a genuine leap of faith when I took my first bite… just a quarter to start with. I eyed up the grey/green yolk, which is the least appetizing colour of anything edible that I can actually think of, closed my eyes and put it in my mouth expecting it to taste how I imagined – disgusting and rank. I waited for my gag reflex to kick in, resulting in me puking my guts out instantaneously. But to my surprise and relief, it tasted nothing close to the flavour profile I had conjured up in my head.

So trust me on this when I say that if you like eggs, you will like century eggs. They have a very intense eggy flavour, great texture and eat particularly well with anchovy, capers and mayo, or anything that complements eggs in general. We put century eggs on with anchovy mayonnaise during the first weeks of opening **BAM**. I'll admit that intimidating diners held some appeal, but I also knew that like me, people would be pleasantly surprised if they gave them a go. I was encouraged by the number we sold – but that might've been due to the fact that we only had six items on the menu. I prefer to think it's because people come to **BAM** to give new things a try.

SERVES 4
2 century eggs
4 heaped tablespoons Anchovy Dressing (page 198)
handful mustard cress
large handful Crispy Pig's Skin (page 91) seasoned with only salt and pepper
dash of Lemon Oil (page 198)

Fill a small saucepan with water, bring to the boil, and add the century eggs. Boil for 6 minutes. Remove from the heat and chill the eggs completely in iced water. Once cold, peel the eggs and cut each in half, cleaning the knife every time you cut through an egg.

Put a spoonful of Anchovy Dressing on four shallow serving bowls and nestle half a century egg on top. Cut a tiny bouquet of mustard cress and pop it next to the egg. Lay some Crispy Pig's Skin next to the egg. Drizzle the cress with a little Lemon Oil and serve.

CRISPY PIG'S SKIN AND BURNT LIME

You are probably bored of hearing the same spiel about getting ingredients from your butcher, giving them notice so they can obtain certain products and so on, but they really are your only point of call if you want certain bits that you can't find in supermarkets, and there's also a good chance that the quality of the meat is going to be higher. Pig's skin is something you'll more than likely have to ask for and rarely see on the counter. Most of the local butchers I've dealt with over the years are happy to help out, and mostly enjoy sourcing more unusual or seldom-requested items and are genuinely interested in hearing about what you're doing with them. There are few things more tantalizing than a bowl of crisp pig's skin. This method won't produce puffy *chicharon*-style skin. Instead, this will give you a more traditional British pub-style pork scratching.

ESSENTIAL EQUIPMENT
food processor or spice grinder
deep-fat fryer

SERVES 6–8 AS SNACKS
1 kg/2¼ lb pig's skin with a little fat (the larger the pieces the better) or 6 pig's ears, or a mixture of both
vegetable oil, for deep frying
plain (all-purpose) flour, for dusting
salt

FOR THE SEASONING
3 dried black limes, lightly crushed
65 g (2½ oz/½ cup) chicken stock powder (bouillon)
½ teaspoon caster (superfine) sugar
¼ teaspoon cayenne pepper or chilli powder

Place all the ingredients for the seasoning in a spice grinder or food processor and blitz to a fine powder. Store in a dry place, in an airtight container. It will last for about 4 weeks.

Place the skin in a large saucepan, cover with water and bring to the boil. Drain the skin, fill the pan once more with fresh water, season with salt and bring back to the boil. The seasoning is important. I generally get the water as salty as seawater. Bring the skin back to the boil one more time then reduce to a simmer. Cut a circle out of baking (parchment) paper that fits snugly inside the saucepan (a cartouche) and place it on top of the skin. Weigh them down slightly with a plate or tray – if the skin is in any way poking out during the cooking, it'll get tough and can't be used, so make sure it's nice and snug. If the pan has a lid, place it on top. If not a double layer of aluminium foil. The foil will actually work better as it allows little or no steam to escape, reducing the cooking time a little. Simmer for 2 hours. After this time, check the skin, but be careful of the steam build up when removing the foil or lid. Poke the skin with a skewer – if it goes in and out with the very slightest resistance, it's done. You can leave it to cool in the cooking liquid and transfer when cold, but I like to chill the skin as soon as possible by running under the cold tap until cool enough to handle.

The skin will be quite delicate at this stage. Lift it out of the water and place skin-side down on a clean dish towel or cloth. Pat the fatty side of the skin with a towel until dry, and gently dry the ears, if using. Layer between squares of baking paper to prevent the pieces sticking together and refrigerate overnight, or for as long as you can before cooking. This makes them way easier to manage and portion.

Once chilled, it's time to slice the skin. Place skin-side down on a chopping (cutting) board and slice as thinly as possible. If you are using ears, place with the tip pointing away from you, and thinly slice vertically.

Heat the oil in a deep-fat fryer to the maximum heat available. Lightly dust the skin slices with flour, then place small handfuls in the fryer basket and lower into the oil. Give the oil a minute to stop bubbling, then lift the meat out. They have a tendency to stick together, so use the tongs to separate the pieces and then lower into the oil once more. Repeat this again a minute or two later. I'm reluctant to give you an exact cooking time as each of you will be using a different capacity fryer that will perhaps have a different maximum temperature or recovery time. I would shoot for 6–8 minutes, checking and separating every couple of minutes.

The skin can look done before it's actually achieved its maximum crunch. When you think the skin is done, take a piece out, place on the towel, allow to cool a bit then take a nibble. They should have a satisfying snap and crunch quality. If they're chewy then they'll need more time in the fryer. Repeat until all the pieces are cooked. Drain on paper towels and allow to cool.

In a big bowl, toss the pig pieces with a generous smattering of the seasoning. I love how the skin looks all heaped up in a bowl. Best served with beers and tequila.

CRISPY FUCKIN' RABBIT

This dish from start to finish is all Tristram Bowden (aka Trick), one of the best chefs I have ever had the privilege to work with. It bridges **BAM**'s transition into a zero-genre restaurant where we can put whatever we like on the menu. We sell colonies of Crispy Fuckin' Rabbit weekly, it's one of the tastiest dishes we sell and it's well worth putting in the effort to make this at home for friends if you have the time. I would encourage you to get ahead by cooking and pressing the rabbit a couple of days in advance of serving it, so the meat is well set and firm when you crumb and cook it.

ESSENTIAL EQUIPMENT
casserole dish (Dutch oven)
2 x 1.3 kg/3 lb loaf pans
weights, such as tin cans
digital thermometer

MAKES 10–12 PIECES

FOR THE RABBIT
1 large rabbit, jointed, offal trimmed (you can ask your butcher to joint the rabbit)
sunflower oil, for roasting and deep frying
8 plump cloves garlic
125 ml (4¼ fl oz/½ cup) white wine
200 ml (7 fl oz/scant 1 cup) dark chicken stock (broth)
100 g (3½ oz/1 stick plus 1 tablespoon) butter
400 g/14 oz lardo in one large piece
200 g/7 oz chicken livers, trimmed
¼ bunch flat leaf parsley, roughly chopped
1 teaspoon Dijon mustard
1 teaspoon grape must mustard
salt

FOR THE COATING
100 g (3½ oz/2 cups) panko breadcrumbs
50 g (2 oz/scant ½ cup) plain (all-purpose) flour
3 eggs, beaten

TO SERVE
2 tablepoons black peppercorns and 2 tablespoons salt, blitzed to a fine powder
4 tablespoons Pickled Mooli (page 201)
1 x quantity Apple and Chilli Sauce (page 198)
lime quarters

Preheat your oven to 160°C/325°F/Gas Mark 3.

Coat the rabbit pieces (minus the offal) with a smattering of oil and season with salt. Put a large casserole dish (Dutch oven) over a medium heat and flash fry the rabbit until golden for 8–10 minutes, adding the garlic for the last 2 minutes. Deglaze the pan with the white wine. Add the chicken stock (broth) and butter, bring to a bubble and nestle in the lardo. Cover the dish with a layer of baking (parchment) paper and a double layer of aluminium foil, cover, and steam for 1–1½ hours, until the meat just starts to come off the bone. Leave covered and allow to cool.

When the rabbit is cool enough to handle, flake the meat from the bone (do not shred). There are a few tiny bones so keep a careful eye out. Remove the skin from the lardo (if necessary) and dice into 1 cm (½ inch) cubes. Meanwhile, reduce the cooking liquid by half. Mix the lardo and the rabbit together in a large bowl, then pour over the cooking liquid.

Set a frying pan (skillet) over a high heat and fry the rabbit offal and chicken livers until they are just cooked, around 3 minutes. Allow to cool slightly and roughly chop. Collect all the juices from the chopping (cutting) board and add them to the meat mixture. Mix in the parsley and mustard and taste for seasoning.

Line a 1.35 kg (3 lb) loaf pan with baking paper. Spoon the rabbit mix into the loaf pan, cover with more baking paper, place the second loaf pan, base-side down, into the pan, and weigh down with tin cans or metal weights – remember this has to fit into your refrigerator – and press down evenly. In addition, if the rabbit isn't pressed hard enough it'll flake apart when it comes to portioning and frying. Refrigerate for at least 8 hours, preferably overnight.

Turn the rabbit out of the pan. If it's reluctant, put the pan in a sink of hot water for a few seconds to loosen the fat a bit. Lay the pan on its side and coax the rabbit out using the baking paper. Whatever you do, don't start slamming the pan against your work surface, as you run the risk of the rabbit breaking apart. Slice the terrine into 12 equal-sized pieces. If they are a little soft, pop them in the refrigerator until they firm up.

Place the breadcrumbs, flour and eggs into three separate dishes and line a baking sheet with baking paper ready to receive the crumbed bunny fingers. With your left hand, flour the first finger. Shake off any excess flour. Using your right hand toss the finger in egg. Place the eggy finger in the crumb. Use your left hand to coat the finger in crumbs and place on the baking sheet. It might sound a little patronizing me telling you what hand to use and where, but it is way cleaner to use dry floury fingers to toss whatever you happen to be crumbing than both fingers being covered in egg, which will pick up more and more crumbs. Once all 12 fingers are crumbed, chill for 1 hour.

Heat a decent glug of oil in a frying pan over a medium heat and fry the fingers for 4–5 minutes, or until golden and crisp on all sides. Alternatively, heat a deep-fat fryer to 160°C/320°F and fry in batches. You are looking for an internal temperature of 75°C/165°F. Drain on paper towels, sprinkle with the salt and pepper mix and serve piping hot, with the Pickled Mooli, Apple and Chilli Sauce and fresh lime on the side.

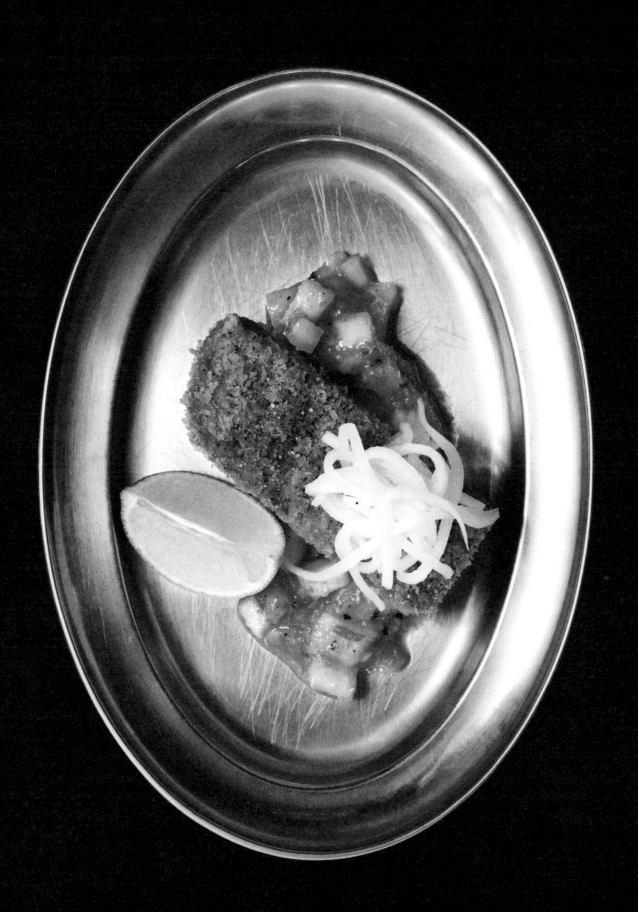

PRESSED OCTOPUS AND SZECHUAN VINAIGRETTE

This dish is one of the more aesthetically pleasing items on the menu at **BAM**. We set the octopus once poached so that when we cut a slice, the octopus resembles marble or terrazzo. Pressing isn't essential so don't stress out if you don't have time or can't be bothered. If you can be bothered, however, you will need two interlocking 450 g (1 lb) loaf pans. Octopus isn't that cheap, so take care when cooking.

ESSENTIAL EQUIPMENT
2 x 450 g (1 lb) interlocking loaf pans
weights, such as tin cans

SERVES 4

FOR THE OCTOPUS
1 large Galician double-sucker octopus,
washed and cleaned
1 leek, roughly chopped
1 teaspoon fennel seeds
1 teaspoon whole black peppercorns
2 bay leaves
1 lemon
1 tablespoon salt
1 tablespoon light olive oil

TO SERVE
150 g (5 oz/1 cup) freshly podded peas
dash of Lemon Oil (page 198)
1 teaspoon black chilli flakes
1 large handful pea shoots, trimmed at the last
possible moment
50 ml (1 ¾ fl oz/¼ cup) Szechuan Vinaigrette
(page 199)
sea salt flakes, to taste
75 g (2¾ oz/½ cup) Turmeric Pickled Onions
(page 200)
4 tablespoons deep-fried baby anchovies
(see method on page 115)

Place the octopus in a deep saucepan and cover with water. Add the rest of the octopus ingredients, apart from the oil, then bring to the boil. Reduce to a simmer, and, using a cartouche (a circle of baking/parchment paper that fits snugly on top of the saucepan) weighed down with a plate, keep the octopus submerged. Cook for roughly 1 hour, depending on size, until poking the octopus with a skewer meets minimal resistance. Allow to cool in the cooking liquid until you can comfortably handle the octopus.

Place the octopus on a large chopping (cutting) board and have a quick scout for any fennel seeds or peppercorns and discard them. Cut the tentacles away from the body then slice off a piece to taste for seasoning, adding a touch of salt if required. We discard the head as the texture is pappy – it's small and tends to overcook. Transfer the tentacles to a bowl and toss the tentacles in the light olive oil.

Line one loaf pan with a double layer of cling film (plastic wrap). Lay the tentacles lengthways and fold over the cling film, placing the second pan (bottom-side down) on top. Press with a heavy weight, such as a tin can, and leave to set in the refrigerator overnight. This will last for 3–4 days.

Cut the pressed octopus into slices and arrange on a platter. Dress the peas with the dash of Lemon Oil and the chilli flakes, and lastly mix in the the pea shoots.

Shake the Szechuan Vinaigrette vigorously then apply generously over the octopus. Sprinkle over a pinch or two of sea salt flakes on top and heap the pea salad on top. Spike the salad with slithers of vivid-yellow Turmeric Pickled Onions, and finally scatter over my favourites, the crispy deep-fried baby anchovies.

SHRIMP-ENCRUSTED PIG'S TAILS WITH PICKLED CHICORY

A happy pig means a pig with a tail intact. Docking is a practice undertaken in industrial farming to prevent overstocked, bored, frustrated pigs from mutilating each other in baron, crowded environments. It's banned in certain countries, but docking can still be carried out in intensive farming conditions if it's deemed beneficial to the pigs' welfare. Sounds fucked to me, but if, like me, you eat bacon, enjoy a fry up on occasion or buy your pork from a supermarket, the chances are that the pig you're eating either had its tail removed by a human or a fellow pig. Buying full-length tails is one way of knowing that the pig has been reared with respect.

ESSENTIAL EQUIPMENT
deep-fat fryer

SERVES 2-3
6 ethically sourced pig's tails
1 tablespoon Dijon mustard
2 eggs, beaten
1 x 100 g/3½ oz bag of dried baby shrimp (Jefi Gold
Pack or Jeeny's brand)
50 g (2 oz/¼ cup) sesame seeds
250 g (9 oz/5 cups) panko breadcrumbs
200 g (7 oz/1¾ cups) plain (all-purpose) flour
vegetable oil, for frying
salt

FOR THE PICKLED CHICORY
3 star anise
1 cinnamon stick
500 ml (17 fl oz/generous 2 cups) white wine vinegar
250 g (9 oz/1¼ cups) caster (superfine) sugar
4 heads chicory, quartered

Infuse the aromatics for the chicory in the vinegar by gently simmering for 10 minutes. Dissolve in the sugar and allow to cool. When completely cool, put the chicory in an airtight container and pour over the pickling liquid. This will keep for several weeks in the refrigerator.

The day before you want to eat the tails, bring them to the boil in a saucepan large enough to accommodate them comfortably. Drain and replace the water, bring back to the boil, add some salt and reduce to a low simmer. Cover the tails with baking (parchment) paper and weigh them down with a small plate so that they are completely submerged. If the pan has a lid, pop it on. If not, cover with a double layer of aluminium foil. The whole point of this dish is to keep the tails intact while cooking the flesh and meat enough to eat it off the bone, which means not cooking them as much as you would a braise. Simmer for 1 hour – they will probably need longer, but I like to check them early so I can gauge how long I think they will take to finish cooking. Use a skewer to poke the fattest part of one of the tails – you're looking for a little, but not total, resistance... a soft resistance. When the tails are cooked, run them under the cold tap until cooled. Refrigerate in an airtight container overnight, until you're ready to crumb.

To prepare the crumb, combine the mustard and the eggs in a shallow bowl large enough to accommodate a pig's tail. In a separate bowl, toss the shrimps, sesame seeds and the breadcrumbs together.

Tip the flour into a bowl and dust the tails in it. Lift each tail out of the flour, gently tap any excess flour off and place the tails into the egg and mustard mix, then toss in the shrimp crumb. The crumbs and sesame should occupy the spaces on the tail the shrimp don't. Each tail should be completely encrusted with shrimp and sesame breadcrumbs. Place on a baking paper-lined sheet and repeat with the rest of the tails. They can be fried immediately or refrigerated until needed, and will last crumbed in the refrigerator for about a day.

Heat the oil in the deep-fat fryer to 160°C/325°F. Lift the basket of the fryer out of the oil and place a couple of tails into the basket then lower them into the oil. Cook for about 6 minutes, until golden and crispy. If using a digital thermometer, they should reach an internal temperature 75°C/165°F. Remove from the fryer and drain on a paper towel-lined baking sheet. Repeat with the other tails.

When all of the tails are fried, place the chicory on plates or a serving platter and the tails on the side.

Pick up the tails and gnaw on them, corn on the cob-style.

PIG'S CHEEK AND PRUNE DOUGHNUTS

The cheeks of a pig are for me the most prized part of the animal. The head in general makes for excellent eating, but a pair of nice fat jowls is the icing on the cake. Most decent butchers will be able to source these with a bit of notice. I first smoked pig's cheeks in Copenhagen during BAM's second week at Bakken nightclub. Well... I say 'I', Tom Adams, who was chef/patron of the original Pitt Cue in London came over to pull me out of the shit and cook with us for a weekend. I brined the cheeks for Tom and when he arrived we smoked them in batches in the tiny electric smoker Tom had lent us for the pop up – the same smoker we use in the restaurant today, still on indefinite loan. It was love at first bite. Sounds corny, but I'm a corny kinda guy.

The first ever Smoked Pig's Cheek and Prune Doughnut made its debut appearance as part of a collaborative barbecue with Marco Frappier, Matty Matheson, Derek Dammann and myself at the enchanting Le Vin Papillon in Montreal. It was important to me that I come up with something unique for this; I'd never actually made the dish before so I was a touch nervous as to how it was going to turn out. The smoking of the pig's cheeks and the frying of the doughnuts were so well executed by Marco and his team that all I really had to do was make the prune purée and take all the credit.

You can cook the doughnuts and smoke the meat a day or so in advance, storing both in airtight containers, so that all you have to do is fry the cheeks and whip up the purée when you are ready to eat.

ESSENTIAL EQUIPMENT
smoker (see pages 50–51)
hand (immersion) blender or food processor
boning knife
non-stick or well-seasoned frying pan (skillet)

SERVES 10
1 x quantity Smoked Pig's Cheeks (page 52)
vegetable oil, for frying
10 BAM Doughnuts (page 196)
sea salt flakes

FOR THE PRUNE PURÉE
400 g (14 oz) prunes, pitted
125 ml (4¼ fl oz/½ cup) brandy or whiskey

📷 P100/101

Once you've made the Smoked Pig's Cheeks following the method on page 52, you'll need to chill them, so during this time, make the prune purée. Soak the prunes in the brandy or whiskey for 1 hour, or more, if you have time.

Once soaked, pour the alcohol and prunes into a small saucepan. Bring to a simmer then allow to cool. When cool, pulse with a hand-held (immersion) blender or in a food processor until you have a rough purée. Store in an airtight container in the refrigerator until ready to serve – this will last for several weeks, so don't worry if you don't use it all.

Next, prepare the cheeks. Secure a chopping (cutting) board to a work surface with a damp dish towel and have your boning knife, or else a small, sharp knife, ready. Pig's cheeks are fatty, so please be careful to make sure the knife handle doesn't get too greased up and become dangerous. To trim the skin, slip the tip of the knife about 2 cm (¾ inch) under the skin and tilt the blade ever so slightly up, directing the knife away from you, and cut nice clean strokes, removing the skin and leaving as much of the fat on the cheek as possible. The smoked skin makes excellent dashi and can add that rich smokiness to stocks (broths), if you're so inclined. Once the skin is removed, flip the cheeks and remove the gland – if it's still attached – and discard. Scan the surface of each side for hairs, removing any you find, then start slicing across the larger part of the cheek, known as the oyster; 2–3 cm (¾–1¼ inch) slices is about right.

Heat a non-stick or well-seasoned frying pan (skillet) over a medium–high heat. Add a glug of oil to the pan and start to fry the pig's cheeks. Cook for 3–4 minutes, until the meat forms a nice crispy surface. Once all the slices are golden and crisp, cook for another 3–4 minutes on the other side.

Cut each doughnut in half using the lighter coloured ring in the middle of the doughnut as your guide. Spread a generous layer of prune purée on each side and sprinkle liberally with sea salt flakes – this adds a little texture and offers another layer of salinity to balance the extreme sweetness of the doughnut and prune. Stack one or two slices of crispy pig's cheek onto the bottom half of the doughnut and secure the top with a cocktail stick or skewer of some description.

You are going to look like a complete bellend if you attempt to eat this doughnut – or any doughnut, for that matter – with a knife and fork. Would you eat a burger or a sandwich with a knife and fork? Hopefully your answer to that is no, so please apply the same logic here. Serve immediately with a pile of napkins and good coffee, or preferably a White Russian.

FOIE GRAS AND BLACKBERRY DOUGHNUTS

I always wanted to do a foie gras doughnut and had talked about it for ages without actually doing anything about it. One day, I came in to the restaurant and Tristram had made a torchon and doughnuts. We put it on the menu that night with Luxardo cherries (which makes an excellent substitute if you can't be bothered to make the compote here) and it became an instant **BAM** classic.

Blackberries grow wild throughout the **UK** when in season, and I have always gone picking, first with my mum and now with my kids. This compote not only goes well with the rich foie gras, but it invokes memories of pink fingers and stuffing myself with berries on the way home.

ESSENTIAL EQUIPMENT
exta-wide cling film (plastic wrap)
butcher's twine
digital thermometer
ice bath

MAKES 10
1 x 500–600 g/17½–21 oz lobe foie gras
1 tablespoon flaky salt, plus extra to serve
25 ml/¾ fl oz whiskey
10 BAM Doughnuts (page 196)
black pepper

FOR THE BLACKBERRY COMPOTE
500 g/17½ oz (4 cups) blackberries
4 tablespoons sugar

📷 P100/101

First make the torchon. Remove the foie gras from the refrigerator and let it get to room temperature, then remove the packaging. You will need to separate the two lobes of foie gras. You should see a red vein running between the two – gently lift the vein and use a spoon to remove the foie. Leave as much of the foie behind as you can. If you end up with lots of bits of foie instead of one big lump that's OK – you can squish it together and reform it. Season the foie all over with the salt and a good grind of black pepper and put it into a bowl in which is fits snugly. Pour over the whiskey and leave to marinade for 10 minutes.

Put a roll of cling film (plastic wrap) in front of you and pull out a very large piece (about 50 cm/20 inches) and fold it in half back towards the packet. Place the foie in the middle of the doubled-over cling film and tip over any juices from the bowl. Fold the cling film over the foie and roll it into a tight sausage shape. Use a tooth pick to stab at any air pockets and push out the air. Tighten up the ends of the sausage and keep pulling out more cling film and rolling it over the torchon to create a smooth log that is roughly the same circumference as the doughnuts. You should use about 10 layers.

Use butchers twine to secure both ends very tightly. I find that wrapping the twine around a few times helps to keep it tight and secure.

Fill a large saucepan with water and bring to a simmer. Use a digital thermometer to measure the water temperature, taking it to 50°C/120°F. Poach the torchon for 10 minutes, making sure to keep it submerged just below the surface of the water. You can also use a water circulator set at 50°C/120°F.

After 10 minutes, remove the torchon and put it immediately into an ice bath. Once chilled, remove and hang in the refrigerator until completely cool.

To make the compote, combine the berries and sugar in a saucepan over a low heat and cook for 10–15 minutes, stirring occasionally to prevent catching. When the juices have leached from the fruit, let it bubble and reduce until sticky, about 10 minutes more. Remove from the heat and refrigerate until needed.

When you are ready to serve, remove the compote and torchon from the refrigerator. Unwrap the torchon and slice the it into finger-width rounds.

Halve the doughnuts, using the lighter coloured ring in the middle of the doughnut as your guide. Heat a griddle pan or dry frying pan (skillet) over a medium heat and toast the doughnut halves for 1–2 minutes until a good char has been achieved. Sprinkle the foie with salt and place on a doughnut half, top with a tablespoon of the blackberries and juices and top with another doughnut half. Eat with your hands.

PLATES

CRUNCHY PRESERVED LEMON SALAD

This is less a recipe than a suggested combination of raw vegetables that eat well together. The clean freshness of this salad cuts through rich food, so it works well with Lamb Offal Flatbread (page 160) or Crispy Fuckin' Rabbit (page 92), amongst many other recipes, but it's also excellent with a simply grilled fish. A mandoline is very helpful for this, but if you don't have one, then a sharp knife is essential. Just watch your fingers.

ESSENTIAL EQUIPMENT
mandoline or very sharp knife

SERVES 4–6 AS A SIDE
2–4 preserved lemons, plus 1 tablespoon of the brine
2 kholrabi, peeled, halved and finely sliced
½ small white cabbage, finely sliced
6 Brussels sprouts, outer leaves removed
and finely shredded
1 bunch breakfast radishes, trimmed and finely sliced
handful chopped kale
100 ml (3½ fl oz/scant ½ cup) olive oil
sea salt

Quarter the preserved lemons and remove all the pips. Slice each quarter into thin strips. Now cut lengthways into the smallest dice you can manage. If the dice aren't that small run your knife through a few times for good measure. It doesn't have to be perfect just very finely chopped.

Put all the vegetables into a large mixing bowl. Toss in the preserved lemon, the brine and the olive oil.

Preserved lemons vary in salinity from brand to brand. I often find I don't need to add any salt whatsoever, but if you feel it needs a little seasoning go ahead and add a pinch of good quality sea salt.

Allow to sit for 10 minutes, then serve.

WATERMELON AND PICKLED GINGER

Watermelon is at its absolute best in the peak of summer, which is around the end of June and throughout July in Europe – the difference in flavour speaks for itself. This salad was inspired by Zak Pelaccio's Fatty Crab, and is great with crunchy pork.

ESSENTIAL EQUIPMENT
mandoline or very sharp knife

SERVES 4–6 AS A SIDE DISH
100 g (3½ oz/½ cup) demerara sugar
200 ml (7 fl oz/scant 1 cup) rice wine vinegar
200 g/7 oz ginger, peeled and julienned
with a mandoline or sharp knife
1 kg/2¼ lb watermelon, chopped into
2.5 cm (1 inch) chunks
2 tablespoons fermented salted black beans
½ bunch Thai basil, leaves picked
black and white sesame seeds

📷 P105

In a small saucepan over a low heat, dissolve the sugar in the vinegar. Put the ginger in a small bowl and then pour over the pickling liquid. Allow to sit for at least 1 hour.

Place the watermelon in a bowl to catch any escaping juices. Mix in the black beans and 2 tablespoons of the ginger pickling liquid.

To serve, pile the watermelon onto a platter, scatter over the pickled ginger and top with the Thai basil leaves and a sprinkle of black and white sesame seeds at the very last minute.

GRILLED HISPI CABBAGE
WITH FERMENTED SHRIMP BUTTER

There exists a gentleman know as Perm, aka The Skinny Bib, who has influenced the menu at BAM in many ways. A confidant during the opening of the restaurant and a provider of exotic ingredients, Perm smuggled anything he thought we would find interesting back from his travels. Perm came back with a kilo of shrimp paste after one such trip, which I thanked him for and then ignored its existence in the walk-in refrigerator. I was making dough at the restaurant and sorting out the refrigerator when I rediscovered the paste. I pulled off the lid and gave it a sniff. I was expecting it to stink... which it did in a way. But the funk of fermented shrimp was mellowed beneath a complex, sweet aroma that reminded me of Parmesan. The paste was too potent and gritty to eat by itself, so I blended some paste into butter. The creaminess of the butter married perfectly with the paste. I was always anxious about putting new things on the menu during the first few months of opening, so I tested the butter with the other chefs. The butter was definitely different and full on. Would customers like it? That was a question I began asking less and less. This dish went on the menu because we knew it was tasty, unique to our restaurant and we were into it. We decided that confidence in *our* palette and gut is what would make us interesting and drive us forward.

This dish is delicious on its own, but it makes an excellent accompaniment to grilled or roasted lamb, beef or pork. The butter can be used for resting grilled meats or fish in, is a solid substitute to Gentleman's Relish, and when spread on bread, makes very fine toast soldiers to dip into a soft-boiled egg. Half a hispi cabbage grills so well, and it's boat-like quality accommodates the butter perfectly, but any seasonal greens would work well with this, such as cavolo nero, purple sprouting broccoli or a bit of bok choy. This makes more butter than you need, and it will keep well in the refrigerator for 12 days. Katsuobushi flakes are dried, fermented, paper-thin pieces of tuna that are rich in umami flavour. You can find them easily online or in Asian supermarkets.

ESSENTIAL EQUIPMENT
hand-held (immersion) blender
barbecue (see page 43) or griddle pan

SERVES 4
2 hispi cabbages, halved
2 tablespoons butter, melted

FOR THE FERMENTED SHRIMP BUTTER
250 g (9 oz/2¼ sticks) unsalted butter,
at room temperature
2 teaspoons high quality shrimp paste
25 g/¾ oz katsuobushi (bonito) flakes,
plus extra to serve
fish sauce, to taste

Blitz the butter ingredients with a hand-held (immersion) blender until smooth, then use straight away or transfer to an airtight container and chill until needed. This will keep for 2 weeks in the refrigerator, but I doubt it'll last that long.

Blanch the cabbage for 2–3 minutes in a saucepan of boiling water. Shock in ice water and drain completely in a colander or large sieve.

If the fermented shrimp butter is in the refrigerator, remove so it can soften a little to a spreadable consistency. Prepare your barbecue following the off-set method (see page 43), or put a griddle pan over a medium–high heat.

Lightly coat the cut side of each cabbage with a little melted butter and grill on zone 2 of the barbecue or cook in the griddle pan. A little flare up from natural charcoal will add to the flavour. When the cut side of the cabbage is good and black, sit it cut-side up on zone 3 of the grill to cook through, about 5 minutes, or turn the heat down to medium–low if using a griddle pan.

Smear the butter over the cut side of the cabbage with the back of a spoon, encouraging it to occupy the gap between each leaf. I suggest using an obscene amount of it, but it's up to you. Finish with a scattering of katsuobushi flakes and serve immediately. It's kind of cute as the katsuobushi 'waves' when it meets the heat.

CHARRED SWEETCORN AND SMOKED COD'S ROE BUTTER

Vegetables and butter served in the most simplistic way are delicious, achievable and classic, so much so that I don't think people stop to think about what a truly great combination it really is. Raised in a large Irish Catholic family, butter and vegetables (mainly cabbage) featured heavily in my diet as a kid. I'd watch a generous knob of butter melt and descend a mound of boiled greens and carrots to be served with buttery mashed potato and boiled bacon. It's still one of my all-time favourite 'Mum' dinners, and on my list of potential death row meals.

The cod's roe in the butter here adds a little extra interest. Smoked cod's roe is salted and cold smoked, which extends its shelf life, but more importantly makes it utterly delicious; you can find it online and at fishmongers. It freezes extremely well, too, so if you don't use it all now it can be saved and used at a later date, or for the Squid Ink Flatbread with Smoked Cod's Roe (page 154).

ESSENTIAL EQUIPMENT
barbecue (see page 43) or griddle pan

SERVES 6
120 g/4 oz smoked cod's roe
200 g (7 oz/1¾ sticks) unsalted butter,
at room temperature
fish sauce (optional)
6 sweetcorn cobs, husks removed
vegetable oil, for grilling
black pepper

First, remove the membrane from the roe as best you can. Spoon the roe into a medium bowl and add a tablespoon of butter. Using the back of the spoon, press the butter into the roe to encourage it to loosen up and separate. Keep adding the butter a tablespoon at a time until the roe is incorporated; the butter should have all the salt it needs from the roe, but taste it just in case. If you feel like it needs to be amped up a bit, add a dash or two of fish sauce. This can be used immediately or kept in the refrigerator. Bear in mind that when it comes to smearing over the sweetcorn it should be around this consistency and temperature, so you'll need to factor in time to bring it to room temperature again before you serve.

Cook the sweetcorn in a large pan of salted water for around 6 minutes. Remove from the boiling water and shock in cold water until cool.

Coat each ear of corn with a touch of oil and cook on zone 2 of the barbecue (see page 43) or in a griddle pan over a medium–high heat, turning the corn every now and again so you've got a nice amount of char on all sides, 3–5 minutes.

Place the sweetcorn on a serving platter then slather with the soft butter, finish with a grind of black pepper and eat.

BROAD BEAN FALAFEL

I hate this dish. At best my relationship with falafel was one of tolerance through lack of imagination. But mostly, I resented falafel for exposing my inability to create a world-class vegetarian option. It was one of the most popular dishes we ever put on the menu at Black Axe Mangal, and people still ask about it now. I was elated when we finally took it off and I solemnly swear that this dish will never, ever – and I mean never – appear on a **BAM** menu again. If you make this recipe, please do not hit me up on Instagram with pictures of it.

ESSENTIAL EQUIPMENT
hand-held (immersion) blender or food processor
deep-fat fryer

SERVES 6
150 g (5 oz/²/₃ cup) dried broad (fava) beans
150g (5 oz/²/₃ cup) dried chickpeas (garbanzo beans)
4 plump cloves garlic, minced
2 tablespoons Bakken Spice (page 197)
1 teaspoon baking powder
1 tablespoon salt
3 spring onions (scallions), roughly chopped
1 large handful equal parts lovage, mint and flat leaf parsley, leaves picked and roughly chopped
1 litre (34 fl oz/4¼ cups) sunflower oil

FOR THE CRISPY PUY LENTILS
50 g (1¾ oz/¼ cup) puy lentils
salt

FOR THE LOVAGE EMULSION
MAKES 350 ML (12 FL OZ/1½ CUPS)
2 egg yolks
1 bunch lovage, roughly chopped
1 handful parsley, roughly chopped
1 teaspoon Dijon mustard
300 ml (10 fl oz/1¼ cups) sunflower oil
squeeze of lemon juice
salt

TO SERVE
1 head frisée lettuce, leaves separated, washed and dried
Lemon Oil (page 198)
black or red chilli flakes, to taste
100 ml (3½ oz/generous ½ cup) natural yogurt
4 teaspoons sumac
small bunch mint, leaves picked
small bunch flat leaf parsley, leaves picked
small bunch dill, torn or roughly chopped
small bunch chives, torn or roughly chopped
Pickled Red Cabbage (page 200)
1 handful guindilla peppers

Soak the broad (fava) beans, chickpeas (garbanzo beans) and the puy lentils (for the crispy lentils) in separate bowls, in plenty of cold water, for 8 hours, preferably overnight. Once the pulses have swelled, drain well and put the beans and chickpeas in one bowl, and the lentils in another. Using a hand-held (immersion) blender or food processor, whizz some of the bean and chickpea mix to a purée and leave some a little chunkier; you will end up with the majority of the mix somewhere between rough and smooth, giving the falafel decent texture when cooked, and also helping to bind the mix when shaping.

If you're making the crispy puy lentils, drain the lentils well, then leave in the sieve over the sink for 1 hour, shaking and tossing every now and again. Things will get interesting if you cook wet lentils in hot oil.

Take a golf ball-sized amount of the bean and chickpea mixture in your hand and form a ball. Does it hold its shape? Yes? Great. Once you have a ball-able consistency you can add the other ingredients. Add the garlic, Bakken Spice, baking powder and salt into the bowl and mix together, then stir in the spring onions (scallions) and the chopped herbs. It's a good idea to chill at this point for 30 minutes to make the laborious job of shaping the falafel that little bit less painful.

Lay a sheet of baking (parchment) paper on a baking sheet, then ball up the falafel any way you want, but no bigger than a golf ball – if you make them too big, they won't cook in the middle. Cover with cling film (plastic wrap) and keep in the refrigerator while you prepare the other components.

Make the lovage emulsion. In a small bowl or in the cup attachment of a hand blender, blitz the yolks, chopped lovage, parsley and mustard together. I've found that my hand-held blender is particularly useful when making small batches of aïoli and mayo. Pour in the oil a little at a time. Lastly season with a pinch of salt and a squeeze of lemon. Store in an airtight container in the refrigerator for up 3 days. Don't worry too much if you're left with little leafy flecks of green visible in this emulsion. If you can't lay your hands on lovage then tarragon is a worthy substitute.

Pour the oil into a deep-fat fryer and set the temperature to 160°C/325°F. Cook the lentils in one batch until golden, around 2 minutes. Drain on paper towels and season with salt.

Preheat the oven to 110°C/225°F/Gas Mark ¼. With the deep-fat fryer still set at the same temperature, fry the falafel in manageable batches until golden brown, around 4–5 minutes, keeping them warm in the oven as you cook the rest.

Dress the frisée in a couple of glugs of Lemon Oil and some chilli flakes. Spread the lovage emulsion over a large platter. Place the falafel on top of the emulsion, then add the yogurt. Sprinkle with the sumac. Heap the salad on top along with the herbs, Pickled Red Cabbage and guindilla peppers. Scatter over the crispy lentils, then serve.

SMOKED MUSSELS

Your clothes will smell wonderful after you've cooked these mussels.

ESSENTIAL EQUIPMENT
barbecue (see page 43) with lid or cloche
large metal bowl or roasting pan
perforated barbecue frying pan (skillet)

SERVES 6
2 bunches samphire, sea beet, purslane
or any other sea greens
1 tablespoon Seaweed Powder (page 197)
70 g (2¾ oz/¾ stick) butter
1 kg/2¼ lb mussels, cleaned and debearded, any open
mussels discarded
10–12 fennel twigs, roughly pencil sized
1 bunch thyme, dried and separated into 2 bundles
2 large handfuls hay, rolled into fist-sized balls

Get the barbecue good and hot. The mussels pop pretty quickly over the heat, so I prefer to cook them in two batches as my perforated barbecue frying pan (skillet) only really accommodates 500 g/1 lb 2 oz, or thereabouts, of shellfish at a time.

In a large saucepan of boiling water, lightly blanch your chosen sea greens, about 30 seconds, then drop into a bowl of iced water to stop them cooking further. Once cool, drain and set aside.

Mix the seaweed powder into the butter in a metal bowl or roasting pan large enough to accommodate all the mussels. Melt the butter in the bowl over the barbecue and then set aside.

Huddle the mussels together in the perforated frying pan, much like nesting Emperor penguins. Place the fennel twigs and thyme on the barbecue followed by the hay. Put the pan directly over the smouldering bundle and immediately cover with the barbecue lid with the vents open, or with a cloche. The smoke will swirl around the mussels while the heat pops them open. The juices will spit and give a little flare up. When the mussels are open (discard any that don't), tip them into the bowl or roasting pan and toss them in the seaweed butter. Throw in all of the sea greens at this point. Repeat the same process with the second batch of mussels then serve.

GULL'S EGG, CAVIAR
AND SEA URCHIN

The absolute pinnacle of my career was on **25 June 2017**, when Black Axe Mangal collaborated with St. JOHN Restaurant at the mothership in Smithfield, London. We were the first restaurant St. JOHN invited to cook in the kitchen in its illustrious **25**-year history. Head chef Jonathan Woolway, Fergus Henderson, Trevor Gulliver and Clan **BAM** collaborated on each course for a one-off menu to feed **120** people. I wanted to create Fergus' perfect bite: sea urchin, gull's egg and caviar was a natural combination.

The urchin is from Kyushu in Japan, harvested in the summer when southern Japanese sea urchins are at their peak; the urchin is then preserved in sake and bottled. This was kindly smuggled back to the UK by our old mate Perm, aka The Skinny Bib. It's the most intense sea urchin flavour I've tasted. Spreading this on some warm bread straight from the grill is sublime; it's only improved by the introduction of an egg, especially one as rich as a gull's egg. For the St. JOHN feast we had no choice but to extend the sea urchin into an emulsion due to the numbers we were feeding. The budget didn't allow for actual caviar either, so we used caviar husks, which are the shells that are left behind when the eggs are removed. I first came across these when I cooked with Dan Barber at his wastED residency at Selfridges department store, London. Caviar husks are absolutely delicious, but hard to obtain. It's difficult to fathom why such an amazing byproduct is left to waste. As I understand it, it comes down to logistics and transportation. I never had the courage to ask how much the gull's eggs cost Jonathan to get in, but I do know they normally go for **£8** [**$10**] a pop, and are only available in the UK for **3–4** weeks of the year. The use of great soy sauce makes all the difference; it helps to season the emulsion but also adds a depth that sea salt lacks.

I know that **50** portions sounds like a lot, but you can't make a smaller quantity of the sea urchin and get everything to emulsify. On the night, I couldn't bring myself to make this through fear of fucking it up, so I decided to leave it in Trick's capable hands – and I still back out of this job. It might actually be impossible to replicate this dish exactly. However, you can recreate the flavours by supplementing the preserved urchin for fresh sea urchin, the gull's egg for half a duck egg or a quail's egg, and the caviar husks for actual caviar… winning.

ESSENTIAL EQUIPMENT
hand-held (immersion) blender
piping (pastry) bags

SERVES 50

FOR THE SEA URCHIN EMULSION
150 g/5 oz preserved sea urchin
50 g/2 oz egg yolks
250 ml (8 fl oz/1 cup plus 2 tablespoons) sunflower oil
1 scant tablespoon best quality soy sauce

TO SERVE
50 gull's eggs
1 x tin caviar, as a big a size as you can afford
gold leaf, to decorate

📷 PP116/117

Tip the sea urchin into the beaker of a hand-held (immersion) blender. Add 1 tablespoon water to the beaker and shake vigorously to free every last particle of urchin.

Add the egg yolks and blend. Slowly incorporate the oil into the egg and urchin. When the oil has been emulsified, blend in the soy sauce. Transfer the emulsion into piping (pastry) bags and refrigerate until needed.

Next, boil the eggs – you'll need to cook these in batches of 10. The eggs are cooked straight out of the refrigerator, so keep them chilled until you are ready to cook.

Bring a large saucepan of water to the boil, then remove from the heat and submerge the eggs into the water. Turn the heat back on and boil the eggs for 6 minutes. After this time, transfer the boiled eggs to a bowl of iced water and allow to cool for 5 minutes.

Line a tray or plastic container with white paper towels (anything with a dye can sometimes impart a stain on the eggs), peel each egg and store in the refrigerator until needed.

When you are ready to serve, allow the eggs to come up to room temperature – 10–15 minutes should be enough. Snip the end off the piping bags with the urchin emulsion and pipe about the equivalent of a heaped teaspoon onto a plate. Pop the egg on top of the emulsion and top with a generous (as generous as you can afford) dollop of caviar. Finesse with a little gold leaf for comedy value and serve. This must be consumed with a maximum of two bites.

BROWN BUTTER POACHED SALT COD, GEM LETTUCE, XO SAUCE

This is another collaborative dish from the St. JOHN and Black Axe Mangal banquet.

Browning butter, or making *beurre noisette*, as it's often called, is easy enough, you just have to pay attention to what you're doing. The theory behind brown butter is to brown or toast the milk solids, which will give colour and flavour to the fat.

Dried baby anchovies remind me of the little scraps of McDonald's fries I used to find at the bottom of the bag. They don't seem to have too many of those scraps in their fries anymore... is it my imagination, or have McDonald's employed a more efficient French fry-cutting system?

ESSENTIAL EQUIPMENT
airtight container large enough to fit the cod
coffee filters
deep, wide saucepan

SERVES 4

FOR THE COD
4 tablespoons sea salt
peel of 1 lemon
4 cloves garlic, minced
1 tablespoon sunflower or vegetable oil
400 g/14 oz boneless cod or white fish fillets, skin on

FOR THE TOMATOES
3 tablespoons olive oil
1 tablespoon sherry or red wine vinegar
4 medium tomatoes or 10 cherry tomatoes, halved
2 cloves garlic, thinly sliced
pinch of salt
pinch of caster (superfine) sugar

FOR THE BROWN BUTTER
500 g (1 lb 2 oz/4½ sticks) unsalted butter

FOR THE SALAD
sunflower oil or vegetable oil, for frying
100 g (3½ oz/1 cup) dried baby anchovies
2 tablespoons Aïoli (page 198)
2 tablespoons XO Sauce (page 199)
2 heads baby gem lettuce, leaves separated
4 spring onions (scallions), finely sliced
2 tablespoons capers

📷 P116/117

First, prepare the cod. Mix the salt with the lemon peel, garlic and oil. Rub the mix all over the fish on the flesh side. Place in an airtight container and refrigerate for 4 hours.

While the fish is in the refrigerator, slow roast the tomatoes. Preheat the oven to 110°C/225°F/Gas Mark ¼. Pour the olive oil and vinegar onto a baking sheet and place the tomatoes cut-side down onto it. Turn them back over and lay one or two slices of garlic on the face of each tomato half. Sprinkle with the salt and sugar then slow roast for 1–1½ hours, until softened and shrivelled, but retaining their structural integrity. Set aside, saving the cooking juices for the salad.

Put the butter into a saucepan over a low heat. Allow the butter to melt undisturbed until it has separated. The solids will start sinking to the bottom. Once the butter starts to bubble, give it a little stir to lift any solids off the base of the pan. Let the butter continue to froth while you keep scraping the solids from the base of the pan. You should start to smell a sweet toffee aroma. If the butter has taken on the colour of beer, it's sufficiently browned. Remove from the heat, allow to cool slightly and pass into a bowl through a sieve lined with a coffee filter to catch the brown bits. Set aside until needed.

Lightly rinse the fish under cold water to remove the salt. Heat the brown butter in a deep saucepan that will fit all the fish in one layer. Place the fish skin-side down and over a low heat, lightly poach for 8–10 minutes – you'll see the colour change from a raw white to an opaque white. At this point, carefully flip the fillets using a fish slice and cook through for another 3–5 minutes, depending on the size of your fillets – you want to take it to the point where it's just beginning to flake apart. Remove the fish from the butter with the fish slice and transfer to a plate, skin-side up. Test the fish by pushing down on the fattest part with a spoon – it should be firm but yielding. Remove the skin by lifting it from one end of the fillet and gently peeling it back. Discard the skin then break the fish into flakes. Repeat with the rest of the fillets. Put to one side or refrigerate until needed. If you do refrigerate to eat later, then heat the butter and warm the fish through in it before serving.

Next, cook the baby anchovies. Frying them is going to make your house, your clothes and your hair stink. You can avoid that by baking them – they will be saltier this way, but still delicious. If you opt for the first method, heat 5 mm (¼ inch) oil in a frying pan (skillet) and shallow fry the anchovies until they turn the colour of French fries, around 5 minutes. Remove from the oil and drain on kitchen towel. To bake, cook in a 110°C/220°F/Gas Mark ¼ oven for 4–6 minutes until crispy.

Mix the Aïoli and XO Sauce with the cooking juices from the roasted tomatoes in a large bowl. Toss the lettuce leaves through the dressing. Mix the tomatoes in with care, then add the warm cod. Move the leaves through your fingers to just incorporate the fish without breaking it up too much. Pile the leaves on a serving platter, spoon a couple of tablespoons of warm brown butter over the salad and scatter the spring onions (scallions) and capers on top. Finally throw the crispy anchovies all over the salad and serve.

SMOKED EEL AND HORSERADISH SQUID INK STEAMED BUNS

Smoked eel will forever remind me of Jeremy Lee and his Smoked Eel Sandwich at Quo Vadis restaurant in London. While we are on the subject of Quo Vadis, if you're looking for exemplary food and service you can't go wrong here. Jeremy Lee and the Hart Brothers are doing great things at QV, and have been for some time.

These buns are me wanting to show off. I thought the two coloured doughs would look really cool (and they do), but it falls into the chef ego bracket, so if you can't be bothered, just combine the two recipes together without the turmeric or squid ink. It will still taste as a good.

Substitute the smoked eel for smoked mackerel if you can't get hold of it. And use lazy horseradish if there is no fresh horseradish available.

ESSENTIAL EQUIPMENT
stand mixer
25 cm (10 inch) three-tier bamboo steamer

SERVES 4-6

FOR THE SALTED LEEKS
2 large leeks, washed and sliced into
2.5 cm (1 inch) rounds
1 handful sea salt flakes

FOR THE TURMERIC DOUGH
125 g (4½ oz/generous 1 cup) strong bread flour
¼ teaspoon baking powder
¼ teaspoon salt
1 tablespoon caster (superfine) sugar
½ tablespoon turmeric
¾ teaspoon fast-action dried yeast
2 tablespoons whole (full-fat) milk
½ teaspoon vegetable oil, plus extra for oiling

FOR THE SQUID INK DOUGH
125 g (4½ oz/generous 1 cup) strong bread flour
¼ teaspoon baking powder
¼ teaspoon salt
1 tablespoon caster (superfine) sugar
¾ teaspoon fast-action dried yeast
2 tablespoons whole (full-fat) milk
1 tablespoon squid ink
½ teaspoon vegetable oil, plus extra for oiling

FOR THE FILLING
5 tablespoons Horseradish Cream (page 198),
or more if you like it fiery
300 g/11 oz smoked eel, cut into 10 slices
50 g (2 oz/½ stick) butter, melted
25 g (1 oz/½ cup) snipped chives

📷 P120

First, prepare the leeks. Tip into a bowl and mix with the salt. Transfer to an airtight container and leave sitting at room temperature for a minimum of 24 hours, and a maximum of 48 hours. After this time, you can keep in the refrigerator in an airtight container for up to 4 weeks; the idea is to give the leeks a little of that fermented tang.

Next, make the turmeric dough. Place the flour, baking powder, salt, sugar and turmeric in the bowl of a stand mixer. Add 70 ml (2½ fl oz/scant ⅓ cup) warm water to the yeast, stir and leave to dissolve for 5 minutes. Mix the yeasty water with the milk and the oil and pour into the stand mixer bowl. With the paddle attachment on the lowest speed, knead for 12 minutes. This slow speed mimics the kneading process if someone was doing this by hand. You should end up with a fun looking mustard yellow ball of dough. Lightly oil a mixing bowl then transfer the dough to a bowl and wrap very tightly in cling film (plastic wrap). This will prevent the dough drying out. Place in a cool spot while you prepare the squid ink dough.

To make the squid ink dough, place the flour, baking powder, salt and sugar in the same bowl of the stand mixer – the ink will soak up the colour of the turmeric, so you don't need to wash it. Add 70 ml (2½ fl oz/scant ⅓ cup) warm water to the yeast, stir and leave to dissolve for 5 minutes. Mix the yeasty water with the milk, squid ink and oil and pour into the stand mixer bowl. With the paddle attachment on the lowest speed, knead for 12 minutes. Lightly oil a mixing bowl then transfer the squid ink dough to a bowl and wrap very tightly in cling film.

Retrieve the turmeric dough bowl and place both bowls in a warm, dry place for 1–1½ hours, until both doughs have doubled in size. The dough should feel smooth, elastic, and be very satisfying to handle once proved.

When the doughs are ready, scoop the balls onto a clean, dry work surface. Stretch each piece of dough into a 15–17 cm (6–6½ inch) length. Wind the doughs together – the more times the better, as this will create the marbling aesthetic. Weigh out 40–45 g/1 ½–1¾ oz lumps of dough – you should have 10 pieces of dough. Now roll each lump into a ball on the work surface by pressing and cupping until you have something roughly resembling a ping pong ball. Allow to rest for 5–10 minutes under a damp cloth, or 20 minutes in the refrigerator if you can spare the space.

While the dough is resting, cut ten 7.5 cm (3 inch) squares of baking (parchment) paper to steam the buns on.

When the dough has rested, use a rolling pin (a smaller rolling pin works better for this) to roll the first ball into an oval shape. Lightly coat the side facing upwards with oil then fold in half so that it looks like a mini bao bun. Stroke a touch more oil on the top, put the bun in the middle of the paper square and place it directly into the baskets of the bamboo steamer. Repeat with the rest of the dough, but don't pack the bao into the baskets like sardines – they will need room to prove and they expand when steaming. I fit 4 comfortably into each tier at home. The advantage of the second prove in the steamer is that they are ready they go directly over the saucepan to cook. Once all of your bao are rolled and nestled into your steamer, wrap the individual baskets in cling film so they are airtight. Prove for 20–30 minutes until the buns have increased in size by about half and are looking plump.

To steam the bao, fill a saucepan that fits the steamer to around a third full with water and bring to a simmer. When it's time to cook, carefully unwrap the baskets and place them on top of each other and pop the lid on. Increase the heat so the water is at a gentle rolling boil with a good amount of steam and cook for 12–14 minutes. Once cooked, turn the heat off and lift the baskets from the pan then leave to cool for 5 minutes with the lid still on – do not attempt to touch or remove the buns before this time as they will be too hot to handle. After the cooling time, you can either serve straight away or allow them to cool completely, then cover.

Drain the leeks and squeeze out any excess liquid. Untangle them a little and mix with the horseradish cream in a small bowl.

At the same time, warm the eel in a frying pan (skillet) over a low heat with the melted butter for 1–2 minutes. You just want to take the chill out of them. If the buns are cold, reheat them by steaming for 5–6 minutes.

When ready to serve, open the buns and brush the insides with a little of the butter from the eel pan. First add the eel and then the horseradish and leek mix, followed by the chives. Serve immediately.

PIGEON WITH BLACKENED ONIONS

The advantage of the set-up at **BAM** is the proximity of the grill to the oven, so using both is effortless. This whole dish can be made indoors without a grill, but the onions won't have that smokey lick.

ESSENTIAL EQUIPMENT
large, heavy-based, cast-iron frying pan (skillet)
digital thermometer

SERVES 2 AS A MAIN COURSE, 4 AS A STARTER
4 medium onions or large shallots, peeled
and halved lengthways
sunflower oil, for frying
4 tablespoons pomegranate molasses
4 tablespoons fermented turnip juice
2 plump wood pigeons (squab), cleaned (ask your
butcher to do this)
50 g (2 oz/½ stick) butter
1 handful flat leaf parsley, roughly chopped
seeds from ½ pomegranate
2 tablespoons Lemon Oil (page 198)
25 g (1 oz/¼ cup) pistachios, toasted
salt

 P121

Preheat the oven to 130°C/260°F/Gas Mark 1, and if you are using the barbecue for the onions, heat using the off-set method (see page 43).

In a mixing bowl, toss the onions with 1 teaspoon oil and a generous pinch of salt. This will hold the salt to the onion and help the onion caramelize before blackening rather than a dry burn, which happens without the appropriate lubrication. Char the onion in a heavy-based frying pan (skillet) or griddle pan over a high heat, or, if using, on zone 1 (see page 43) of the barbecue. Tip the onions into a roasting pan, sprinkle over the molasses and the turnip juice and roast in the oven until the onions have softened but still have a little bite, around 15 minutes. Set aside somewhere warm while the pigeon is cooking.

Season both pigeons with a little salt. In a heavy-based, preferably cast-iron frying pan (skillet) large enough to accommodate both pigeons and give you enough room for basting, heat 1 tablespoon of oil and place the birds in the pan leg-side down. Fry for a minute or so before tossing in three quarters of the butter. The butter will hiss and froth. I like to tip the pan a touch and almost deep fry the legs in the 'well', where the base meets the side. Do this for about a minute and repeat with the other leg. Like most birds, the legs take a little longer to cook, so it's good to take them that bit further before they go into the oven. Turn the birds onto their backs, tip the pan again to create the 'well' and spoon the bubbling butter over the breast of the bird until the skin is a rich bronze colour, about 3 minutes.

Drain the butter from the frying pan and place the pan in the oven for 6 minutes. After that time, check the internal temperature at the fattest part of the pigeons' breasts with a digital thermometer – it should read at around 55°C/130°F, so if it doesn't, keep cooking. Once done, rest somewhere warm with the remaining butter for a further 3 minutes.

To carve the birds, place one of the pigeons on a chopping (cutting) board with the breasts facing you. Bridge the bird with your non-dominant hand, thumb on one breast and fingers on the other to hold in place on the board. Slip a sharp knife under the bridge and slice through the first 2 cm (1 inch) of flesh on that side of the breast plate. Hug the ridge of the breast plate with your knife following the natural line as a guide until you reach the wishbone. Take your knife down and cut through the wing joint. Spin the bird 180 degrees and cut the flesh from the bone using the tip of the blade and your fingers until you reach the leg socket. Pop the leg socket and remove the breast and leg from the carcass. The breast you see before you should be red-wine coloured and blushing. Repeat with the other breasts. Pop back into the frying pan, cover with aluminium foil and rest for 5 minutes in the butter and cooking juices.

Pile the onions on a platter and scatter over the parsley and pomegranate seeds. Arrange the pigeon breasts around them. Tip the butter and resting juices over the meat, followed by the Lemon Oil and lastly, scatter with the pistachios. Serve immediately with steak knives.

BUTTERMILK FRIED CHICKEN WINGS WITH MISSION CHINESE CHONGQING SPICE

Who likes KFC? Just me? Okay. Let me ask you that in another way. Who likes fried chicken? Not liking fried chicken is like never seeing *Star Wars*. I don't know any meat eater who doesn't like fried chicken. For reference, watch the fried chicken episode of 'Ugly Delicious' (which to my mind is second only to the pizza episode). We've served fried half chickens and half guinea fowls at the restaurant, but there is something so perfect about the chicken wing. It's grabbable, gnawable and succulent. Don't try to eat these with a knife and fork like a weirdo.

Mission Chinese Chongqing spice originates from one of my favourite restaurants in the world, Mission Chinese Food, owned and run by my friend Danny Bowien. Danny has had a significant impact on me as a chef, and on our restaurant.

ESSENTIAL EQUIPMENT
deep-fat fryer
digital thermometer

SERVES 4
12 x 3 joint chicken wings, wing tips removed
40 g (1½ oz/2 tablespoons) fine sea salt
8 cloves garlic, minced
1 litre (34 fl oz/4¼ cups) buttermilk
sunflower or vegetable oil, for deep frying
500 g (1 lb 2 oz/4½ cups) plain (all-purpose) flour, for dusting
3 tablespoons Mission Spice (page 197)

TO SERVE
4 tablespoons Tahini Sauce (page 198)
4 tablespoons Aïoli (page 198)
50 g (1¾ oz/½ cup) shop-bought crispy fried onions
1 tablespoon red chilli flakes
Dill Pickles (page 200), finely sliced
2 limes, quartered

📷 P124/125

Rinse the chicken wings under cold water. Place in a mixing bowl and scatter salt over the wings. Give the bowl a toss to distribute the salt. Add the garlic and the buttermilk to the bowl and mix. Submerge the wings in the buttermilk, cover and refrigerate for a minimum of 8 hours, but preferably overnight.

Once your wings have marinated, fill a deep-fat fryer with oil and heat to 160°C/325°F.

Tip the flour into a large, shallow bowl. Remove the wings from the buttermilk, shaking off any excess liquid, then dredge the wings in the flour. Set aside for 10 minutes, allowing the flour to take to the skin.

When ready to cook, push the flour into all the nooks and crannies, shake the wings free of any excess flour, and place in the basket of your fryer. Lower the basket into the oil and fry for 6–8 minutes, or until the wings reach 75°C/165°F. The best way to determine whether they are cooked is to use a digital thermometer, so I'd recommend investing in one. Drain on paper towels.

Toss the wings in a mixing bowl with the Mission Spice, then arrange on a platter and drizzle the lot with Tahini Sauce and Aïoli. Tip any scraps from the fryer and excess wing spice over the chicken along with the crispy onions and chilli flakes. Serve with the Dill Pickles and lime quarters on the side. A Lagerita (page 188) is particularly good to drink with these wings.

QUAIL WITH SHRIMP SAMBAL

This recipe can easily be scaled up or down to however many people you are feeding. I can crush two easily by myself, but if you want to feed a crowd, a quail's size means they work well as part of a larger meal. I am including both indoor and outdoor methods that give equally good results.

ESSENTIAL EQUIPMENT
barbecue (see page 43), if using barbecue method
mini food processor

SERVES 2-4
4 large quails
2 tablespoons vegetable oil
1 tablespoon salt
6 cloves garlic, thinly sliced
50 g (12 oz/½ stick) butter
fish sauce, to taste

TO SERVE
Shrimp Sambal (page 200)
2 limes, quartered

I prefer to spatchcock quails if I'm grilling on a barbecue. This is easily done by cutting out the spine with a sharp pair of scissors. Cut along the right side of the spine, from the tail to the neck, and then cut along the left side. Remove the spine (you can save it to use in stock if you want) and press the bird down to flatten out into one piece. Leave the quail whole if you are using the pan-frying method.

Prepare the quails by rubbing them with the vegetable oil and then sprinkling with the salt. Put them in a large bowl and toss with the sliced garlic. Cover with cling film (plastic wrap), and leave to marinade in the refrigerator for a minimum of 6 hours, or preferably overnight. When you are ready to cook the quail remove the garlic and season again with a little more salt.

To barbecue the quail, lay each spatchcocked bird breast-side down on the medium hot area on your barbecue following the offset method (page 43). If you can, arrange the legs so they are closest to the coals, as the legs require a touch more cooking, so the extra heat is needed. Give the skin time to acquire some colour and char, around 3 minutes, then flip the bird onto the other side to char. Move to zone 4 (see page 43) of the barbecue to finish cooking for 6–7 minutes, until the breasts feel firm, or until each one reaches 60°C/145°F in the fattest part of the breast. Allow to rest in a roasting pan for 5–6 minutes with the butter and a few dashes of fish sauce, rolling the quail around a bit in the fishy butter.

If you'd prefer to roast the quail in the oven, preheat the oven to 220°C/425°F/Gas Mark 7.

Heat a heavy-based frying pan (skillet) over a high heat. Add a little splash of oil to the pan and lay the whole birds down on their sides. Add half of the butter. Tip your pan and, using a pair of tongs to hold the birds, shallow fry the legs a little. Repeat on the other side with the other leg. Flip over to give the breasts some colour. Transfer to the oven for 4–6 minutes, or until the breast is 60°C/145°F at the fattest part. Remove from the oven, drain the butter from the pan and replace with the other half of the butter and a few dashes of fish sauce. Allow to rest for 5–6 minutes, rolling the quails around in the fishy butter.

To serve, place the quails on a platter, cutting them in half down the length of the breast if you have spatchcocked them, and pour over the butter and resting juices. Put on the table with the sambal and limes on the side. Again, it's a struggle for me to watch people use a knife and fork to tackle a quail, so I suggest having a roll of paper towel handy and encouraging your friends to spoon the sambal onto the quail using their mitts and to gnaw the tiny carcasses clean.

SPICED PLUM AND MALLARD WITH TURMERIC GRABBERS

Mallard season in the UK starts in October and ends around January. Although smaller than a reared duck, the mallard punches above its weight in terms of flavour, which allows us to match it with heavy hitting or spicy garnishes – this will work with duck if you can't find it, though. The grabbers are essentially beer-mat sized steamed buns ideal for dipping, mopping and building little sarnies.

ESSENTIAL EQUIPMENT
stand mixer
6 cm (3 inch) round cookie cutter
bamboo steamer
well-seasoned or non-stick frying pan (skillet)

SERVES 4

FOR THE CONFIT
2 tablespoons grated ginger
2 cloves garlic, minced
½ teaspoon Bakken Spice (page 197)
1½ tablespoons salt
250 ml (8 fl oz/1 cup) melted duck fat or olive oil

FOR THE MALLARDS
2 mallards, legs and breasts separated from the carcass
salt and freshly ground black pepper

FOR THE SPICED PLUMS
400 g/14 oz plums, pitted
1 tablespoon demerara sugar
¼ teaspoon ground star anise
½ teaspoon ground allspice
¼ cinnamon stick
3 teaspoons red wine vinegar
1 teaspoon salt

FOR THE TURMERIC GRABBERS
250 g (9 oz/2⅓ cups) strong bread flour
½ teaspoon baking powder
½ teaspoon salt
2 tablespoons caster (superfine) sugar
1 teaspoon ground turmeric
1½ teaspoons active dried yeast
1 teaspoon vegetable oil, plus extra for greasing
70 ml (2½ fl oz/⅓ cup) whole (full-fat) milk

TO SERVE
2 bunches spring onions (scallions), julienned
1 English cucumber, cut into matchsticks
1 small bouquet of peppery watercress

Confit the mallard legs the day before. Mix together all the ingredients for the confit apart from the duck fat then rub over the legs, place in an airtight container and chill for 4 hours. Rinse, then bring the fat to a bubble in heavy-based saucepan over a low–medium heat, drop in the legs and, using a digital thermometer to check the temperature, cook at 110°C/225°F for 2 hours. The meat should be cooked but not falling off the bone. You can refrigerate the legs now or use straight away.

To make the spiced plums, place all the ingredients in a saucepan and cook over a low heat for about 30 minutes, until the plums are soft but still holding a little of their shape. Remove from the heat then allow to cool. Set aside. This will keep in an airtight container in the refrigerator for up to a week. Make sure the sauce is at room temperature when serving.

To make the turmeric dough, place the flour, baking powder, salt, sugar and turmeric in the bowl of a stand mixer. Add 70 ml (2½ fl oz/⅓ cup) warm water to the yeast, stir and leave to dissolve for 5 minutes. Mix the yeasty water with the milk and the oil and pour into the stand mixer bowl. With the paddle attachment on the lowest speed, knead for 12 minutes. Lightly oil a mixing bowl then transfer the dough to the bowl and wrap tightly in cling film (plastic wrap) to prevent it drying out. Allow to prove until doubled in size, around 1–1½ hours.

While the dough is resting, cut ten 7.5 cm (3 inch) squares of baking (parchment) paper and brush with oil.

When the dough has rested, scoop it out onto a clean, dry work surface and roll out to 1 cm (½ inch) thickness. With the cookie cutter, stamp out as many discs as you can – I average around 10. Put the rounds on the squares of paper and place in the steamer. Don't pack them in – they will need room to prove and steam. Once filled, wrap the individual baskets in cling film. Prove for 20–30 minutes, until they have increased in size by about half and are looking plump.

To steam the grabbers, fill a saucepan to around a third full with water and bring to a simmer. Unwrap the baskets and place them on top of each other and pop the lid on. Increase the heat so the water is at a gentle rolling boil and cook for 12–14 minutes. Once cooked, turn the heat off, lift the baskets from the pan then leave to cool for 5 minutes with the lid on. You can either serve straight away or cool and cover until ready to serve.

When ready to eat, finish preparing the mallard. Lay the legs skin-side down in a well-seasoned or non-stick frying pan (skillet). Cook over a low heat, crisping up the legs gradually. When the skin is crispy, flip and crisp up the other side. The legs can sit quite happily while the breast is cooking and resting.

To cook the breasts, lightly rub each with a dab of oil. Season well on both sides. Lay the breasts skin-side down in the same frying pan over a medium heat. Leave undisturbed for 3 minutes, then flip and cook for a further 2 minutes. Remove from the heat and rest the breasts in the pan for 2–3 minutes.

While the breasts are resting, reheat the grabbers over a low steam, if needed. Slice the rested breasts and arrange on a plate. Place the legs on top and pour over the resting juices. Put on the table with the plums, salad and grabbers. Get stuck in.

A NOTE ON HARE

Hares in general are sold whole. Wild animals are extremely lean, and like all game, benefit from hanging to tenderize the meat and develop their flavour and aroma. The legs and shoulders of a hare need to be braised at a low temperature, whereas the saddle needs only moments on a very hot grill or pan with a decent rest. The length of time the hare has spent hanging will determine how funky the offal might be, but if you are tempted, put it this way – I can't remember the last time I used a liver, kidneys or heart from a hare to make a cheeky treat for the butcher or chef after all that work.

Your eyes and fingers are as important as your knife when approaching any kind of butchery, if you want to do a decent job of it, that is. Anyone can hack up a chicken, but doing it properly requires knowledge, practice and skill. Butchering hares – and rabbits, too – is a straightforward, fun introduction to butchery if you are curious but have little to no experience in that area, so that's why I've included a step-by-step here. Technically speaking, the anatomy of a hare is very similar to a lamb, and I apply the same basic principles when I butcher either – a lamb is obviously just a hell of a lot bigger. My advice is to get organized and give yourself enough time to do this so that you actually enjoy the process, especially if you haven't attempted anything like this before.

—
1
Secure the chopping (cutting) board to the work surface using a damp cloth or damp paper towel. Have three containers ready next to it – one for the legs, shoulders and ribs, one for the saddle, and one for any unwanted trim. Take a moment to use your fingers to feel the lines between the bones and muscles, giving you a guide for your knife.

—
2
Lay the hare on its back on the board. If there is an excess of blood, give it a wipe. Generally speaking, both hares and rabbits will come with their liver, heart and kidneys still attached.

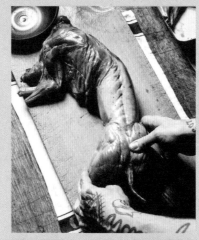

—
3/4
You will notice a thin membrane across the ribcage. Inch your index finger and thumb inside the ribcage and pull out the lungs and heart. It might be a good idea to do this over the trim container as this cavity can hold a lot of blood. Discard everything including the heart. Free the kidneys from the saddle and discard them.

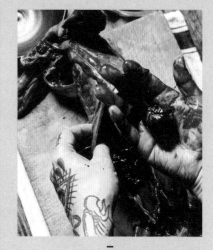

—
5
Put the hare on its side. Give the shoulder a wiggle. Feel around until you locate the shoulder blade.

—
6/7
Push the shoulder down slightly so the shoulder blade is slightly raised, insert your knife through the flesh under the shoulder blade, and with a couple of smooth strokes, separate the shoulder from the carcass. See? Easy, right? Flip the hare and repeat, then place the shoulders in the waiting container.

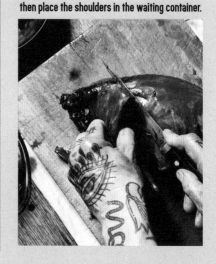

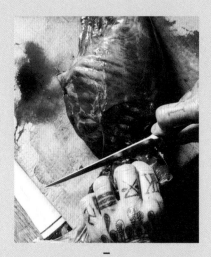

–
8

Next, remove the belly flaps. Put the hare on its back, find where the flap meets the upper leg and follow the natural line between the loin and belly flap until you meet the ribcage. Continue to cut the flap away around the lower part of the ribcage until the flap is free. Repeat. Place the flaps in the container with the shoulders.

–
9

Using a pair of kitchen scissors, snip the ribcage off the carcass along the line where the ribs and the upper loin meet. Keep the bones with the shoulder.

–
10

Have the hare on its back again and move onto the legs. There is an obvious line to follow between the lower loin and the legs. Use your fingers again to find the pelvis bone. Slip your blade in and slit the flesh down through what I would compare to the groin, exposing the ball joint.

–
11/12/13

Pop the ball joint from its socket using both hands and continue to slice away the leg, hugging the pelvic bone and leaving as little flesh behind as possible. Repeat with the other leg and place in the container.

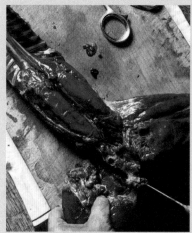

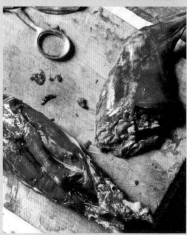

–
14

Remove the pelvic bones by cutting away the connective muscle and pulling them away.

→

15

This will leave a little tail of spine that needs to be chopped off. This last step is important to me. You can just chop the pelvis bones off in one go, squaring off the base of the loin, but that would take some of the loin meat away with it. Remember, anyone can hack up a piece of meat. Pop the bones in the container, cover and refrigerate until you need to braise.

You should be staring at a ruby red dismembered hare loin. The next step is the trickiest part. Removing the skin requires a very sharp knife; a basic goal when butchering an animal is removing bone, cartilage or trim as economically as possible. Start at the base and work up towards the neck end. Insert the tip (3 cm/1¼ inches) of your knife facing the blade away from the spine. Angle the blade up at the slightest of upwards angles so you can see the tip through the skin. Move the knife forwards up the length of the loin using the spine as your guide.

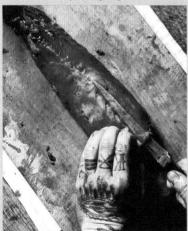

17

When you've got your knife about half way, start cutting towards the chopping board, still keeping the blade at an upwards angle. Cut through the line where the skin and the loin meet. Edge your knife into the loin again, employing the same method all the way until you get to the neck. Repeat this on the opposite side. At this stage you will be left with two flappy bits of skin. Take both flaps in one and remove them by running your knife along the spine from the neck end to the base. Discard the skin. Now for the silver skin. Remove this as best you can – the technique is much the same as above. Discard any snippets of skin. Remove the loin from the spine. Start your incision at the neck end, running the knife all the way to the base, hugging the blade against the spine the whole time. Think about it this way – angling your blade away from the meat reduces the risk of you removing any flesh. Once you've done it a couple of times it'll feel more natural.

18

Now cut under the line at the base and work your way back up the saddle removing the cannon of meat (the fillet from one side of the loin) with a few neat strokes of the blade. Repeat and remove the other cannon. The hare is now ready to be grilled. Keep hold of the spine to roast and boost the flavour of your braise.

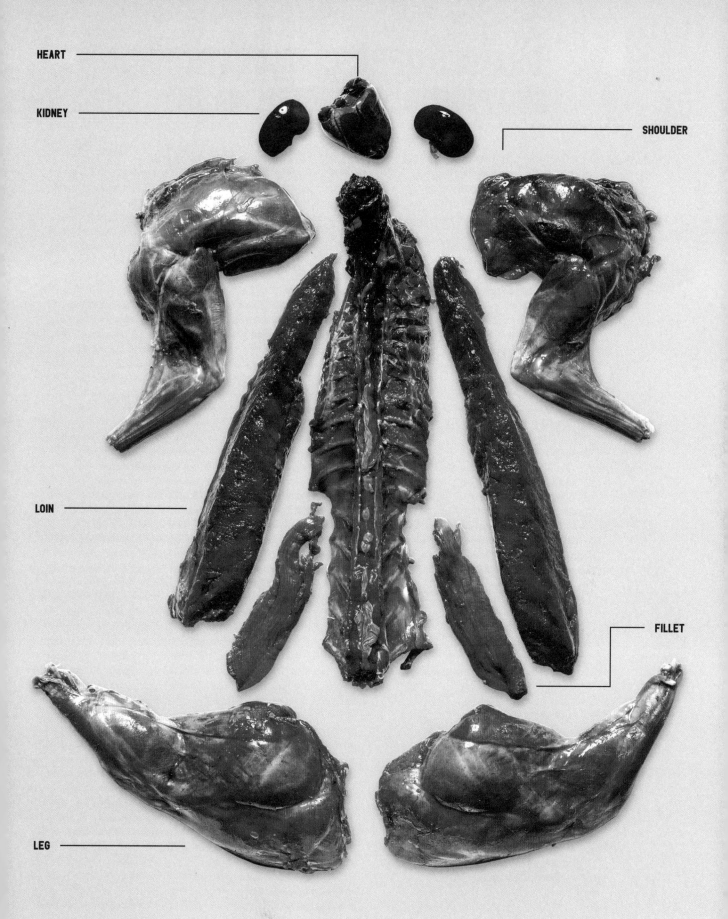

HEART

KIDNEY

SHOULDER

LOIN

FILLET

LEG

BRAISED HARE, CHOCOLATE AND PIG'S BLOOD WITH MASH

Stews and braises are often better the next day. It's not essential to make this a day ahead but if you can it will allow everything to get to know each other. Part of the playfulness of this dish is that it looks like something you'd get in a classic French bistro, but the flavours are classic Chinese – except for the mashed potato, of course.

ESSENTIAL EQUIPMENT
large roasting pan or casserole dish (Dutch oven)
potato ricer

SERVES 2
legs and shoulders of 1 hare (pages 130–133)
ribcage, spine and pelvic bones of 1 hare (pages 130–133)
sunflower oil, for frying
50 g (2 oz/½ stick) butter
500 ml (17 fl oz/generous 2 cups) dark chicken stock
200 g/7 oz lardo or pancetta, diced
240 ml (8 fl oz/1 cup) red wine
1 teaspoon palm or demerara sugar
3 star anise
30 g/1 oz ginger, sliced
1 red chilli, fresh or dried
¼ teaspoon ground cinnamon
20 g/¾ oz 70% cocoa solids dark chocolate
50 ml (1¾ fl oz/¼ cup) fresh pig's blood
(ask your butcher for this; optional)
1 hare saddle, deboned and trimmed (pages 130–133)
1 tablespoon soy sauce
salt

FOR THE MARINADE
60 ml (2 fl oz/¼ cup) sunflower oil
4 cloves garlic, thinly sliced
2.5 cm (1 inch) piece ginger, roughly chopped or grated
salt

FOR THE MASH
1 kg/2¼ lb Yukon Gold or Maris Piper potatoes, peeled and sliced into 2.5 cm (1 inch) pieces
2–3 tablespoons whole (full-fat) milk
300 g (11 oz/1½ sticks) butter, chilled and diced
salt

TO SERVE
steamed greens of your choice
3 tablespoons Fermented Black Beans with Ginger (page 199), room temperature
1 x quantity Pickled Red Cabbage (page 200)

Preheat the oven to 150°C/300°F/Gas Mark 2.

Put the hare legs, shoulders and bones into a large bowl with the marinade ingredients. Cover with cling film (plastic wrap) and let marinate in the refrigerator for at least 6 hours or overnight.

Place a deep frying pan (skillet) over a medium–high heat. Add a generous tablespoon of oil, remove the hare pieces from the marinade, shaking off any excess, then salt the meat lightly and fry. Once the hare has been cooking for a minute or two, add half of the butter, then flip and fry the other sides for the same length of time. The purpose of frying the bones is to enrich the flavour of the braise, and giving these a bit of colour will deepen the flavour. Once browned, place the meat in a roasting pan or casserole dish (Dutch oven). Tip the butter and oil into the pan or dish and return to the heat. Add the stock, deglaze the base and bring to a boil. Once the stock is boiling, toss in the lardo or pancetta. Add the wine to the pan and bring to a bubble. Scatter in the sugar and stir until dissolved. Throw in the star anise, ginger, chilli and cinnamon. Pour over the hare, then cover the dish with the lid, or if using a roasting pan, cover tightly with baking (parchment) paper and aluminium foil. Braise in the oven for 4 hours, or until the meat comes away from the bone.

When the hare is cooked, allow the meat to cool until you can handle it. Taste the braise. If it needs a little salt, add a pinch, but it should be pretty much there with all that salty, fatty pork in there. Discard the carcass bones and pick the meat from the shoulder and leg bones then set aside.

Next, strain the stock into a measuring jug (large measuring cup) – it should be around 300 ml (10 fl oz/1¼ cups).

Pour the stock back into the roasting pan or casserole dish and place over a low heat to warm through, adding the chocolate and stirring until melted. You can either mix the meat back in and refrigerate to serve later or finish the dish by adding the pig's blood, if using, stirring constantly until the stock thickens. If you are refrigerating, to serve, heat the meat and stock until almost bubbling, then allow to cool a little before adding the pig's blood. If you add the blood to the piping hot stock it will curdle, so all that time and effort goes out the window.

Bring a large pan of salted water to the boil and simmer the potato slices until just cooked. Set a sieve or colander over the sink and drain the potatoes, allowing them to sit in the sieve to steam for a few minutes so that they dry out a little. Add the milk to the pan and place over a low heat. Pass the potato through a ricer into the pan then work in the cold butter with a spatula and season well. Keep warm while you cook the hare saddle.

Very lightly oil the hare loins and season with fine salt. Cook in a non-stick frying pan over a seriously high heat for 1–2 minutes. Flip the loins and repeat for the same amount of time, then allow to rest in the other half of the butter and the soy sauce for 2 minutes.

To serve, spoon the mash onto a large platter and add the greens. Top with the hare braise. Slice the loins on a diagonal to a thickness of 1 cm (½ inch) and place on top. Finish with the Fermented Black Beans with Ginger and Pickled Red Cabbage.

BLOOD CAKE FRIED RICE

Once you've made this blood cake you can simply cut it into slices, fry it and eat it with a fried egg and a blob of brown sauce. Job done. At **BAM** we serve it with fried rice… well, we used to. The limitations of our tiny service kitchen made it such a pain in the ass, so we only run it when we are feeling particularly confident and upbeat. I will do more fried rice dishes when we get a bigger restaurant – it's one of the most satisfying things to eat, and I love how versatile fried rice can be. It's also a supreme way of using up small quantities of miscellaneous bits and pieces such as a nub of bacon, smoked pig's cheek, oxtail or octopus, for example. The possibilities and combination are endless. What you add to this rice is entirely up to you. I've suggested wild garlic, but that can easily be replaced with some black cabbage, pak choi or broccoli. It's also important to know that this dish will combat even the most potent of hangovers.

Making a blood cake follows the same principles as making custard. Blood thickens (coagulates) when heated. So it's important to keep the blood moving while you cook it.

ESSENTIAL EQUIPMENT
450 g (1 lb) loaf pan
wok or large well-seasoned or non-stick
frying pan (skillet)

SERVES 6

FOR THE BLOOD CAKE
1 large onion, diced
1 tablespoon vegetable oil
1 tablespoon Mission Spice (page 197)
500 ml (17 fl oz/generous 2 cups) fresh strained
pig's blood
1 teaspoon salt
1 teaspoon freshly ground black pepper
200 g/7 oz back fat, Smoked Pig's Cheek (page 52)
or a combination of both, diced
100 g/3½ oz pearl barley, cooked and cooled

FOR THE SPICED ONIONS
1 large onion, diced
25 g (1 oz/2 tablespoons) butter
1 tablespoon Mission Spice (page 197)

FOR THE RICE
vegetable oil, for frying
2 red or green chillies, sliced
700 g (1 lb 8½ oz/4 cups) cooked white rice
handful of wild garlic
50 ml (1¾ fl oz/¼ cup) fresh pig's blood (optional)
soy sauce
6 duck eggs
Pickled Red Onions (page 200; optional)
Mission Spice (page 197; optional)

Line the loaf pan with a double layer of cling film (plastic wrap) with enough excess to fold over when the pan is full.

Preheat your oven to 110ºC/225ºF/Gas Mark ¼.

In a saucepan large enough to accommodate all the ingredients for the blood cake, cook the onions in a little oil over a medium heat until translucent. Add the Mission Spice and cook for a minute further. Set the heat to low–medium and pour in the pig's blood. Move the blood around, constantly scraping the bottom of the pan with a spatula, until the blood starts to thicken. Continue to cook and stir the blood. It will thicken and noticeably increase in volume. Season with the salt and pepper at this point. At this stage the blood should be ready to receive the back fat – to test that it's at the right point though, drop a cube or two of back fat onto the surface of the blood. If it sinks to the bottom you need to thicken the blood further. If the fat sits comfortably on top of the blood, remove the pan from the heat and mix in the rest of the fat along with the barley.

Transfer the blood to the loaf pan. Wrap the cling film over the blood mix. Place the loaf pan in a deep roasting pan and pour boiling water into the roasting pan around the loaf pan to about three-quarters of the way up. Cover the pans with baking (parchment) paper and aluminium foil, carefully transfer to the oven and bake for 30–40 minutes, until the blood cake is firm.

When the blood cake is cooked, remove from the oven and bain marie and allow to cool. Chill in the refrigerator for a few hours before cutting into it.

Next, make the spiced onions. They provide a sweetness for the rice, but make sure you have them pre-cooked before you start the stir fry so it's simple to throw together at the last minute. In a small frying pan (skillet), cook the onions in the butter over a medium heat. When the onions are translucent, after about 10 minutes, remove from the heat and stir in the spice.

Cut 4 slices of blood cake, then cut each slice into 6 pieces. Get all your ingredients lined up ready to throw in and cook.

Get a wok or large, well-seasoned or non-stick frying pan (skillet) going over a high heat. If you have an extractor fan, I would turn it on now, or open a window.

Lightly oil the pan and fry the blood cake pieces. Allow the blood to fry for a couple of minutes, add the chilli and cook briefly, then chuck in the rice and spiced onions. Let the rice and onions sit and get a little heat for a minute before stirring. The blood cake will break up a bit, but don't worry. When the rice is piping hot, fold in the wild garlic and stir in the fresh pig's blood, if using. Finish with a dash of soy sauce.

Fry the duck eggs. While the eggs are frying, mound the rice on a platter. When the eggs are done, place onto the rice with a few Pickled Onions on the side. I would definitely reach for the Mission Spice at this moment too. Sprinkle some over if you have any to hand. Ice cold cider is an excellent drinks pairing.

BEEF TARTARE ROYALE

I adore prawn (shrimp) toast. The warm, crappy fried white bread, soft sweet prawn and crunchy sesame with a spicy dip pushes all my buttons. I was inspired to make a version after a disastrous prawn toast experience with Trick in a Vietnamese restaurant in Dalston, London, recently. The prawns were heaped onto a round of French baguette studded with sesame. It was a way I've never seen it served before. But my excitement turned to disappointment at first bite. The prawn was raw and cold in the centre and the mix was so dry it separated itself from the bread. The crusts on the bread were fried so hard it was impossible to eat without cutting into the roof of my mouth. Not a lot to be inspired by you might be thinking, but that toast taught me how *not* to prepare and serve this as a dish at the same time as opening my mind and exploring all the different ways I could possibly improve upon it. Sometimes it's just as important for me to know how I don't want a dish to look or taste, and work back from there.

After much research on YouTube and multiple tests trying to make prawn toast steamed buns work, with little success, I concluded what I'd suspected all along – that everyday white bread is by far the best. I made my prawn paste quite wet to adhere to the bread and sesame. My original idea was to use it as the bread for a surf 'n' turf steak sandwich. We made this for a few VIPs and proudly posted it on Instagram, but the sarnie was just too rich and full on... and for Black Axe Mangal to pass on a dish because it's too full on and rich is saying something.

A beef tartare toast sandwich with an egg yolk morphed into the recipe you see before you. Like the Braised Hare on page 134, I love the classic, French brasserie-aesthetic of this dish, and how as a result, the flavours really surprise you.

ESSENTIAL EQUIPMENT
food processor
chef's food presentation ring
deep-fat fryer

SERVES 6

FOR THE PRAWN TOAST
250 g/9 oz raw prawns (shrimp), peeled and deveined
20 g (¾ oz) ginger, chopped
2–3 cloves garlic, chopped
½ bunch spring onions (scallions), chopped
1 egg
3 teaspoons fish sauce
2 teaspoons soy sauce
1 teaspoon sesame oil
6 slices thick-cut white bread
50 g/2 oz dried baby shrimp
1 tablespoon mixed black and white sesame seeds

FOR THE BEEF TARTARE
300 g/11 oz fully trimmed, well marbled, aged beef such as ribeye, rump or fillet
1 tablespoon fermented chilli sauce
2 tablespoons Anchovy Dressing (page 198)
1 shallot, finely diced
1 red chilli, finely diced
1 teaspoon capers, finely chopped
black pepper

TO SERVE
6 egg yolks
25 g (1 oz/¼ cup) Pickled Red Chillies (page 201)
1 punnet mustard cress
50 g (2 oz/½ cup) baby anchovies, fried until crispy (see method on page 115)
sprinkling of Seaweed Powder (page 197)
1 tablespoon black chilli flakes

To make the prawn toast, process the prawns, ginger, garlic, spring onions (scallions), egg, fish and soy sauce and sesame oil into a paste using a food processor or a hand-held (immersion) blender in a beaker. Refrigerate until needed. This can be done in advance but use the mix within 2–3 days.

Slice the beef into 1 cm (½ inch) dice and tip into a bowl. Mix the diced raw beef with the fermented chilli sauce and the Anchovy Dressing. When this is fully mixed add the diced shallot, chilli and capers with a grind of black pepper.

I'm all for family-style dining, but for this dish, I like individual plating. Especially presented in an old-school way using a chef's presentation ring. Place the ring in the middle of the plate and spoon in enough beef to fill the ring to the top. Repeat with the rest of the portions, then make a little divot in the top of each for the egg yolks.

Fire up your deep-fat fryer to 180°C/350°F. This toast can be shallow fried just as well if you don't have a deep-fat fryer. Just make sure you have at least 2–3 cm (¾–1¼ inch) of oil in the pan.

Slather the face of each slice of bread evenly with the prawn paste. Scatter the dried baby shrimp and sesame seeds on top of the paste, securing the shrimp and seeds with a gentle pat. Fry the toasts in batches for 1–2 minutes on each side, until crisp and golden. When fried, drain on paper towels to absorb any excess oil. If you're worried the toasts might get a little cold, keep them in the oven at a low temperature.

Cut each slice of toast in half from corner to corner, giving you two obtuse-shaped triangles. Arrange the toasts either side of the raw beef. Nestle the egg yolks into the divots in the beef and add a pinch of pickled chilli and a tuft of mustard cress next to the yolk. Finish with a few crispy anchovies and a sprinkle of Seaweed Powder and black chilli flakes on top of the yolk.

Use the toast as a vehicle to transport the beef from the plate to your mouth.

ROASTED RUMP CAP

This is as close to a foolproof method as you'll get for cooking rump cap perfectly every time. I always feel like a don if I cook a thick-cut steak perfectly on the grill using only my fingers and judgment as a guide. But for every one I nail, I ultimately over or under cook a good few too. The recipe below will hopefully take the stress out of it for you a bit. I am suggesting rump cap, which is known in Brazil as a *picanha* – basically the top of the cow's ass. I prefer this cut because it's a manageable size and has a decent layer of fat. It's hard to skimp on price when it comes to high-quality beef, so this is a special occasion kind of spend, unless you're minted.

The condiments and garnishes are completely up to you. Lettuce cups were something we put on the menu during week one when I was still trying to figure out what the fuck I was doing and tinkering with the menu constantly. I needed to add lighter dishes to the menu and have always appreciated the convenience of a loaded lettuce cup, whether filled with egg mayo, prawn cocktail or coronation chicken. The crisp cleanliness of the lettuce gives you licence to heap a bunch of mayo, greasy stuff and pickles into the cavity. As long as you have crunchy, warm, cold, crispy and acidic elements, it will be tasty, and personally, I also like a touch of heat. The time the beef takes in the oven is ample time to prepare the garnishes for this feast.

ESSENTIAL EQUIPMENT
barbecue (see page 43)
digital thermometer

SERVES 6

FOR THE MEAT
1 well-aged beef rump cap (about 1.3–1.5 kg/
2¾–3⅓ lb), trimmed
fine sea salt
1 tablespoon beef dripping or vegetable oil (for pan frying)
70 g (2¾ oz/¾ stick) butter
fish sauce, for deglazing

TO SERVE
2 heads baby gem lettuce, leaves separated
1 large or 2 small kohlrabi, peeled and thinly sliced
3 nori sheets cut into beer mat-sized pieces
sprigs of chervil, tarragon or mint
handful freshly podded peas
handful pea shoots
1 small bunch spring onions (scallions), chargrilled and roughly chopped
Buttermilk-fried Shallot Rings (page 197)
small native oysters, as many as you can afford, or as many as you can be fucked to shuck
salmon roe
caviar
1 x packet (100 g/3 ½ oz) dried baby shrimp
Pickled Mooli (page 201)
Pickled Red Chillies (page 201)
Pickled Green Tomatoes (page 201) roughly chopped
Aioli (page 198)
Anchovy Dressing (page 198)

Preheat the oven to 110°C/220°F/Gas Mark ¼.

Season the beef all over with fine salt. This can be done an hour or so before. At this point you can choose to do one of two things to sear the beef. The idea behind both methods is to get a good colour on the meat as quickly as possible, maximizing flavour on the outside and minimizing the cooking on the inside.

If you have a barbecue, you would be mad not to take advantage of the opportunity to sear your beef over the coals. Set up the barbecue following the method on page 43. Turn the meat regularly using tongs, watching out for flare ups from the fat, until you have a beautifully charred hunk of beef. Ever since I stained my kitchen ceiling yellow with smoking beef fat, much to my wife's disapproval, come spring, summer, autumn or winter, I almost always fire up the barbecue to grill my beef as a result.

Otherwise, fry in a heavy cast-iron frying pan (skillet), but make sure there is plenty of room around the sides, as you'll need it for basting. Pat your beef dry as best you can with paper towels or a clean dish towel to reduce any spitting when you place the meat in the pan. Heat the pan until it's smoking hot. Add the dripping or vegetable oil to the pan then add the beef fat-side down – the meat should sizzle and spit. Render the fat a little while keeping an eye on the colour. A light caramel will do at this stage. Turn the beef and add 40 g (1½ oz) of the butter to the pan. Carefully tip the pan at an angle and baste the beef with the frothing butter. Keep turning the beef until the surface is caramelized and the fat is golden.

Once the meat is browned either on the barbecue or in the pan, transfer it, fat-side down, to a roasting pan with a wire rack and cook for 1 hour. After this time, flip the meat and probe the centre though the top of the joint – the target is 51–52°C/123–126°F. Flip the meat each time you check the temperature for an even cook, but try to gauge it so you aren't opening the oven door every 5 minutes. When the meat has reached the desired temperature, rest the joint somewhere warm for 10–15 minutes off the rack, in the roasting pan, with the remaining butter and a few dashes of fish sauce, which should deglaze and lift any juices from the bottom of the roasting pan. Turn the beef over in the butter and juices a few times during resting. If you're feeling brave and you trust me, carve table side in front of your friends and family. If you can't resist, cut a little slice off to reassure yourself.

Serve with your choice of the accompaniments, first placing a slice of beef in the lettuce cup, then adding the toppings.

ADANA SKEWER AND GRILLED TURKISH SWEET CHILLIES

Adana kebabs are named so after the Turkish City of Adana. The Adana are traditionally hand chopped using a *zirh*, a huge crescent-shaped cleaver – a method I've never tried, but would love to have the opportunity to under the tutelage of someone who knows what they are doing. Like most things at BAM, our version is just that. A version. There is no real nod to authenticity involved in our technique – or ingredients, for that matter, as we use pork. I wanted the result to be as amazing as possible, so I chose the tastiest path, as opposed to the most authentic, employing a method I knew worked well.

From what I've seen, Adana kebabs are best cooked using the off-set heat method (page 43) on broad skewers. The Adana skewers at their most basic look like long blades designed to straddle the opposite sides of the grill. Some have points and intricate handles. Needle-like skewers won't hold the meat as well and can be hard to turn on a barbecue, so best to be avoided. In fact, it would be better to use no skewer at all if you don't have the flatter type, or you are having a few difficulties with shaping the meat around them – just form the mix into patties and cook directly on the grill.

It's best to work quickly, keeping the meat as cold as possible so it behaves. If you haven't done this before, it may take a few attempts. I felt like Lion-O, leader of the ThunderCats wielding the Sword of Omens when I held aloft my first Adana... matched equally in my horror as I watched the meat peel off the skewer and land on my shoe.

ESSENTIAL EQUIPMENT
ice
flat Turkish-style kebab skewers
barbecue (see page 43)

SERVES 4–5

FOR THE SKEWERS
500 g/1 lb 2 oz minced (ground) pork back fat, chilled
10 g/¼ oz curing salt
10 g/¼ oz fine sea salt
8 cloves garlic, minced
2 tablespoons Bakken Spice (page 197)
1 kg/2¼ lb lean minced (ground) pork, ideally from the leg, chilled

—

TO SERVE
1 kg/2 lb 3¼ oz Turkish sweet chillies, friggitello peppers or padron peppers
sea salt
Lemon Oil (page 198)
BAM Flatbreads (pages 56–63)
natural yogurt
Sumac Shallots (page 197)
chilli sauce
pomegranate molasses

Have everything weighed out and ready before you start anything. The tray or bowl you're going to mix your meat in should be clean, and it goes without saying so should your hands.

Put the bowl in a large roasting pan and surround it with ice. Place your chilled minced (ground) fat in the bottom of the bowl and season with the salts, garlic and Bakken Spice. Mix well. Add the chilled lean minced meat to the bowl and combine. Mulch and mix the meat and fat between your fingers enthusiastically. This process agitates the proteins that will bind the meat. When the meat and fat are homogenized, start to add 150 ml (5 fl oz/⅔ cup) ice-cold water, a little splash at a time, incorporating each splash fully until all the water is mixed in. The meat should be stickier now. A rule of thumb is when the meat sticks to the palm of your hand, it's ready to go, so keep mixing until you achieve this. Chill in the refrigerator for 1 hour.

Once chilled, divide the mix into 10 equal portions, roll into balls, return to the bowl and chill again in the refrigerator.

Line a baking sheet with baking (parchment) paper. Gather your skewers, fill a bowl with cold water and retrieve the portioned meat from the refrigerator. The skewers need to be bone dry – the meat won't adhere if they are wet. Hold the skewer in your left hand (if you are left-handed hold it in your right), take a ball of meat and squeeze it around the skewer as close to the middle as possible. Wet the same hand and squeeze the meat against the skewer, massaging it towards either end. The water prevents your skin from sticking to the meat, so dip your hand in again if needed. At this stage, just concentrate on getting an even amount of mix distributed along the skewer; it needs to be good and thin, but not so thin that you can see the metal through it. This will decrease the cooking time, and prevent the meat from falling off the skewer. Pinch the meat between your finger and thumb 1 cm (½ inch) from the base to the tip to create the classic pinched, kebab-like shape (see picture), then place on the baking sheet. Repeat with the rest of the meat.

Smoke is an important character to the Adana's flavour. Lay your skewers on the grill of your barbecue just shy of the coolest section (see page 43). Make sure you get a decent bit of char and colour on the meat – this should take 5–8 minutes. If you're feeling confident, remove the grill and have a go at cooking the skewers the authentic Turkish way, balancing the skewer across the barbecue, still in the coolest section, allowing the smoke and an occasional flame to lick the meat.

Cook the chillies directly over the coals until they have a decent char, then transfer to a cooler part of the grill to finish and soften slightly, around 3 minutes. Toss the chillies in a bowl with a good pinch of sea salt and a glug of Lemon Oil.

Pile the meat onto a plate and serve with the chillies and the rest of the accompaniments.

OX HEART DEEPTHROATER

I first tasted ox heart at St. JOHN, and it fast became one of my favourite cuts. I was surprised at how tender and delicious it was. I also loved how quick and easy it was to cook during a busy service. Ox heart is my go-to if I'm having friends over for a barbecue or doing a cooking demo. I've never asked a butcher to prep and slice an ox heart because I'm pretty sure the answer would be a polite no. Prepping ox heart is extremely satisfying if you have time and a sharp knife, a less enjoyable experience if you are short of either of these. In which case, you can fry up minute steaks in much the same way.

You will find *ezme salata* in every Turkish restaurant in some shape or form. Traditionally served as a mezze, its a pretty versatile salsa kind of thing, or a stand alone salad if chopped a little more chunky. Excellent to eat with bread, it reminds me of the Catalan tomato bread, with a bit more complexity. I especially enjoy it with super salty feta and cheap olives – they all balance well and it's a good vegetarian alternative to this.

This dish came about in Copenhagen during our second week at Bakken nightclub. There is a place in Istanbul called Dürümzade, recommended by the late great Anthony Bourdain in his series *No Reservations*. Hands down the best kebab I've ever eaten, I ate there everyday I was in the city. Shout out to Dürümzade. I wanted to insulate the ox heart I was serving and thought a Dürümzade-style wrap would be perfect to help hold that heat in. I also wanted to encourage people to eat with their hands, so wraps seemed like a logical step. This combination of accompaniments also works well with the Adana Skewer (page 142). I use shop-bought hummus because I can't make a good one.

ESSENTIAL EQUIPMENT
barbecue (see page 43)

SERVES 8-10

FOR THE OX HEART
1 ox heart
2 tablespoons vegetable oil
1 tablespoon fish sauce
1 tablespoon red wine vinegar
8 cloves garlic, thinly sliced
a few sprigs thyme
1 teaspoon fine sea salt

FOR THE EZME SALATA
1 large white onion, diced
sea salt
1 tablespoon sumac
1 tablespoon black or red chilli flakes
2 bunches flat leaf parsley, roughly chopped
1 kg/2¼ lb ripe tomatoes, roughly chopped to 2 cm (¾ inch) pieces
4 cloves garlic, minced
4 tablespoons pomegranate molasses
olive oil, for drizzling
juice of 1 lemon

TO SERVE
8-10 BAM Flatbreads (pages 56-63)
shop-bought hummus
Turkish kebab-shop style pickled chillies

📷 P147

Place the heart on a chopping (cutting) board and dab it with paper towel to make it less slippery. It's safer to cut away from yourself when prepping ox heart, so hold the blade with the tip pointing away from you. There will be random slashes in the heart when you get it home from the butcher. Theses are the result of strict health inspections carried out by vets at the abattoir when the cow is dressed. Start by trimming the white fat from the crown of the heart, keeping as much of the meat behind. Cut any hard cartilage away from what would be the top of the heart, then slice into 3–4 palm-sized slabs.

You'll notice a silver skin on the outer side of the heart, and a cobweb-like membrane on the inner side. This is technically edible, but will retract when grilled, and your lovely slices will curl up as a result, so we remove it. Cut away strips of the silver skin as carefully as possible so as not to lose too much of the meat. Flip and remove the inner membrane in the same way. You will find veins of fat along the way that need to be trimmed off as well. Basically, you want to be left with just ruby red pieces of heart.

The next step is slicing. Inspect the trimmed heart. See which direction the grains run on each piece – like any cut of meat, if you slice along the grain it'll be tougher. The muscle structure of a heart is quite complex: the muscle cells swirl around in a figure-eight pattern that enables the heart to pump effectively, so slicing it isn't so straightforward. Cut 1–2 cm (½ –¾ inch) thick slices, or thereabouts, then place in a bowl with the oil, fish sauce and vinegar, then fold in the garlic and thyme. Cover and refrigerate overnight if possible.

For the ezme, mix the onion with a generous pinch of salt, sumac and chilli in a mixing bowl and give it a toss. Add the parsley, followed by the tomatoes and garlic. Mix well, then drizzle in the pomegranate molasses with a glug of olive oil and lemon juice, to taste.

Check the grill is hot (see page 43). Really hot. Season one side of the ox hearts with the salt – it's so thin that you don't want to overdo it. Have a separate bowl ready to receive the ox heart when cooked. Start to grill the ox heart in manageable batches, laying each piece seasoned-side down. When the last piece is on the barbecue, take a peek at the first slice you put on. If there are nice bar marks on the face, flip it. If not, give it a minute. Cook the flipped side for half the time you did the first – you'll be cooking each piece for 2 minutes at most. Place in the bowl somewhere warm and repeat until all the heart is cooked.

To assemble the wraps, reheat the breads on the barbecue. Lay each one on a square of aluminium foil a little bigger than the bread. Start by smearing a healthy dollop of hummus across the bottom quarter of the bread and smatter with the pickled Turkish chillies. Use a slotted spoon to apply the salad so the bread doesn't get overly wet. Load with ox heart and a touch of the resting juices. Lift the lip of the loaded side of the bread into the centre. Gently squeeze the flipped part into itself and roll towards the other side. Roll it too tight and all the juices will be pushed out, too loose and everything falls out. Secure the wrap with the foil. Fold or twist the ends to catch the escaping juices. Cut in half with a serrated knife and serve. This can get messy, so be sure to have lots of napkins handy and maybe don't wear your best chinos.

BAKKEN SPECIAL, THE OG BAM DISH

I seem to recall describing this as a self-lubricating kebab. This was the only dish in the **BAM** repertoire when I went to Copenhagen to do the pop up. The other dishes were born out of sheer desperation. I'd prefer you to eat this the old fashioned way, out of a **BAM** Basic Flatbread. All the textures and flavours and the combination of hot and cold elements balance and compliment each other, however, lentils or bulghur wheat also marry well with this stew.

Smoking the lamb shoulder is not essential for the recipe to work. The smoke undoubtedly adds flavour, especially to the fat, but if you're unable to or just can't be bothered, skip the smoking step and go straight to steaming it in the oven.

SERVES 6

FOR THE BAKKEN SAUCE
12 plump cloves garlic
50 ml (1¾ fl oz/scant ¼ cup) sunflower oil
6–8 large shallots, quartered
150ml (5 fl oz/⅔ cup) liquid from the roasted
red peppers
1 x 1 kg/2¼ lb jar roasted red peppers, drained
and roughly chopped
100 g (3½ oz/½ cup) sweet *biber salcasi*
(Turkish red pepper paste)
100 g (3½ oz/½ cup) tomato puree (paste)
2 tablespoons Bakken Spice (page 197)
80 ml (2¾ fl oz/scant ⅓ cup) pomegranate molasses
80 ml (2¾ fl oz/scant ⅓ cup) fermented turnip juice,
sauerkraut brine or water
2 tablespoons demerara sugar
sea salt

FOR THE LAMB
50 g (2 oz/¼ cup) caster (superfine) sugar
50 g (2 oz/¼ cup) sea salt
50 g (2 oz/¼ cup) Bakken Spice (page 197)
2 kg/4½ lb lamb or mutton shoulder

FOR THE KIDNEYS
6 lamb kidneys, peeled and halved
sunflower oil
50 g (2 oz/½ stick) butter, melted
1 tablespoon black chilli flakes
sea salt

TO SERVE
Pickled Red Cabbage (page 200)
natural yogurt
black chilli flakes
Sumac Shallots (page 197)
fermented chilli sauce
2 handfuls flat leaf parsley, leaves picked
BAM Basic Flatbreads (pages 56–63)

To make the Bakken sauce, choose as wide a frying pan (skillet) as possible. Over a medium heat, fry the garlic in the oil with a pinch of salt until nut brown and softened. Remove the garlic with a slotted spoon and keep to one side for later. Fry the shallots in the garlic oil with a pinch more (about a teaspoon) of salt to a light caramel colour. Deglaze the pan with the reserved juice from the roasted peppers and chuck the garlic back in. Add in all the other sauce ingredients and mix well. Reduce to a low heat and simmer for 20–30 minutes, stirring every now and again to prevent the sauce from catching to the pan. Allow to cool before storing in the refrigerator. This will last for about a week, so it can be done way ahead of the lamb shoulder.

The day before you want to cook the lamb, mix the salt, sugar and Bakken Spice together in a small bowl. Rub the shoulder with a touch of oil, then cover in the Bakken mix. Refrigerate for at least 3 hours, or overnight.

If you are smoking the lamb, follow the smoking method on pages 52–53. Smoke the shoulder for an hour and a half, maintaining a temperature of 110ºC/225ºF.

Preheat the oven to 150ºC/300ºF/Gas Mark 2.

Place the shoulder on a rack set inside a roasting pan with 2 cm (1 inch) water in the base. Cover with baking (parchment) paper and a double layer of aluminium foil, then steam in the oven until the meat is just about falling off the bone. This should take around 4 hours. Rest until cool enough to handle, then separate the meat from the bone in decent-sized chunks and add them to the sauce. Taste the liquid in the pan – if you think it will enhance the sauce, add it in. Chill in the refrigerator until needed – stews and braises benefit from a period of time to mature, so I often make this the day before.

The kidneys are the last thing you need to cook to complete this dish. That means the lamb in the sauce is hot, the bread is freshly grilled or revived over the heat and all your garnishes are ready to serve. Halve each kidney using a sharp knife. You will see each half has a hard white nugget of connective tissue. This is known as the kidney pelvis, and I only know this because I Googled it. Anyway. You have to remove it. Pinch it between your thumb and middle finger and index finger. Cut it away with the tip of your knife and discard.

Lightly oil the kidneys and season with a pinch of salt. Place the kidneys outer side down in a frying pan (skillet) over a medium heat. They will stick if you move them too soon. When the blood starts to show and pool on the cut side, turn over. This a super cheesy analogy, but when I learned to cook kidneys, I was told that they will tell you when to turn them. Cook for a further 30 seconds then rest in a bowl for a minute or two with the melted butter and toss with the black chilli flakes.

Heap the meat and sauce onto a platter, top with the kidneys and juices, then serve with the accompaniments.

FLATBREADS

DELICA PUMPKIN FLATBREAD

I struggled with vegetarian options when **BAM** first opened, and if I'm honest, it's still an area I could dedicate more thought to. Having little sympathy for vegetarians at the time and a growing list of tasks that comes with opening a restaurant, I decided that I didn't have to bother. Kate, who was a vegetarian and vegan for some years, had a deeper understanding than I of the outdated, afterthought attitude that had haunted restaurant menus for decades, and so, as the opening date loomed large, she asked me what the vegetarian options were. At this point I had resorted to a Broad Bean Falafel (page 111), a dish that never sat well with me on the menu, no matter how much people loved it. 'That's it?' Kate said when I told her. 'Yeah, we have a salad, too,' I replied – and the argument I'd practised in my head for not bothering evaporated instantly. I had devoted all my energy to finding lame excuses for why I didn't need to provide vegetarian dishes instead of just concentrating on coming up with strong options. It was the height of pumpkin season, and I'd roasted a couple of Delica pumpkins a few days before in an attempt to conjure up some inspiration. Kate suggested that the pumpkin could work on a flatbread, an idea I dismissed defensively, then snuck off and tried an hour later. I patted out some dough and smeared it with the soft chunks of roasted pumpkin and garlic. Before I even got the bread into the oven, I knew it was going on the menu, and would please anyone who ate it, vegetarian or not.

ESSENTIAL EQUIPMENT
food processor
pizza oven, pizza stone or cast-iron frying pan (skillet)
(see pages 60–62)
2 pizza peels

MAKES 8
12 cloves garlic, peeled
a few sprigs thyme
1 medium Delica pumpkin, peeled and diced
1 small butternut squash, peeled and diced
240 ml (8 fl oz/1 cup) light olive oil
1 x quantity BAM Basic Flatbread Dough (page 58)
salt

TO SERVE
4 tablespoons pumpkin and sunflower seeds, toasted
250 g/9 oz hard cheese such as Old Ford, Berkswell or Sparkenhoe Red Leicester, for grating
toasted pumpkin seed oil (optional)
Lemon Oil (page 198)
black chilli flakes
175 g (6 oz/1 cup) guindilla peppers, roughly chopped

Preheat the oven to 200°C/400°F/Gas Mark 6.

Place the garlic and thyme in a bowl with the pumpkin and squash, a pinch of salt and the olive oil. Toss everything together until the garlic, pumpkin and squash are nicely coated. Transfer onto a baking sheet with any residual oil and a splash of water. Roast in the oven until the edges start to caramelize, and the pumpkin and squash are tender. I like to take it to just bronzed. When done, discard the thyme and any garlic that might have burned. Transfer the pumpkin to a food processor and blend until smooth.

Pat out the first piece of Flatbread Dough following the method on page 60. Once on the pizza peel, smear a heaped tablespoon or so of the squash all over the dough with the back of a spoon. Follow the steps to cook the bread on pages 60–62. The dough should be blackened in places and the squash mixture will have taken on a little more colour.

Remove from the oven with the second pizza peel, scatter over the seeds, grate a stupid amount of cheese over the surface then lace with toasted pumpkin seed oil, if using, but if not, add a little of the oil from the squash. Finally, add a few drops of Lemon Oil for acidity, a pinch of black chilli flakes and a sprinkling of guindillas for a bit of a kick. Repeat with the rest of the dough and toppings and serve.

SQUID INK FLATBREAD WITH SMOKED COD'S ROE

The Squid Ink Flatbread started out without any squid ink at all. Farmer Tom, a friend and long-time supplier came in one night with a group of mates. As usual, I was looking for a way to show off, and wanted to give them something that wasn't on the menu. At the time, the menu had about eight items, and the only extras I had were a few eggs in the walk-in refrigerator. So I decided to blindly experiment with baking an egg onto a flatbread. I quickly found out that isn't as straightforward as I'd anticipated – in fact, the first attempt was an unmitigated disaster. What happens to a raw egg on a raw flatbread a few centimetres from the flame of an oven at about 300°C/570°F is neither pretty nor edible. After a few more failures, though, I started to work things out. The bread has to be cooked first, for starters, and be flat... you might think that's obvious, but I had this great idea I could almost poach an egg in the well of a bun-like flatbread and conceal it so there is a 'surprise egg' when you cut into it. That didn't work. I also discovered that you need to give the egg a bit of lube in the form of olive oil or melted butter, otherwise it just dries out. The final hurdle was the yolk overcooking while the white was still underdone... in the end, separating the yolk and discarding most of the white cracked it. We served this on sesame bread with smoked cod's roe and some Seaweed Powder lifted from a snack that was on the menu for Tom and his friends, and then promptly forgot about that dish. It was only when I made a squid ink dough a few months later that we returned to the idea... after all the experimenting during service that night, which put us well in the shit, we at least had something decent to show for it.

ESSENTIAL EQUIPMENT
blender or food processor
pizza oven, pizza stone or cast-iron frying pan (skillet)
(see pages 60–62)
2 pizza peels

MAKES 10
½ x quantity BAM Basic Flatbread Dough (page 58),
replacing 30 ml (1 fl oz/2 tablespoons)
water for squid ink
10 egg yolks
6 tablespoons butter, melted
10 teaspoons Seaweed Powder (page 197)
edible glitter, to decorate

FOR THE SMOKED COD'S ROE
100 g/3½ oz) bread, crusts removed
250 ml (8 fl oz/1 cup) whole (full fat) milk
500 g/17½ oz smoked cod's roe, peeled
25 g/¾ oz garlic, minced
500 ml (17 fl oz/2 cups) rapeseed/neutral oil
juice of 2 lemons
salt, to taste

Make the Flatbread Dough in exactly the same way as described on page 58 but portion to 90 g/3¼ oz per piece. All you are doing is supplementing some of the water for squid ink. I think it's important to add the Smoked Potatoes (page 196) for this recipe, for the chunky texture, but it will still work without. Keeping one hand free while making this dough is advised even more so than before, given the colour.

To make the cod's roe, soak the bread in the milk for an hour or so. The milk will soften the bread and allow it to become smooth, which gives the cod's roe body and makes for better odds of getting a velvety texture.

Put the soaked bread into a blender or food processor along with the cod's roe and minced garlic. Start the machine on a medium speed for about 1 minute. Increase the speed to medium–high and start incorporating the oil slowly. Adding the oil at a steady pace will prevent the mix from splitting. If your blender starts to labour as a result of the mix becoming thick, add a splash of milk or water to thin it a little. The consistency is very important – you are aiming for something akin to a very smooth hummus, as it has to hold its shape when you spoon it on the finished flatbread. Too thin and the roe will run off the bread; too thick and the roe will clag in the mouth. It's better to have a thicker mix and add liquid until you have the right consistency rather than trying to thicken a sloppy mix. Once you've reached the desired consistency, check the seasoning. If the roe is particularly salty you may get away without adding any additional salt. It will certainly need lemon juice – this helps balance the smoke and salt and ease any bitter edge. Again, just a little at a time until you're happy with the level of acidity. Chill in an airtight container until needed.

Now, cook the breads. If you have access to a pizza oven of some description, fire that thing up. If you only have access to a domestic oven it's okay... Jesus loves you. This bread works either way – the visual impact may not be as aesthetically pleasing, but it'll taste just as good. Follow your preferred method on pages 60–62. Only pat the dough out to 2.5 cm (1 inch) thick and 12.75 cm (5 inches) in diameter.

When you have all your flatbreads cooked, the next stage is to bake the egg yolk on top. Use a teaspoon to make a small dent in the centre. Drop an egg yolk into each dent, then drip some melted butter over the yolks and return to the pizza oven or domestic oven for a final spell. If you fly too close to the sun your wings will melt. Same applies here. Put the breads closer to the cooler side of the oven. After all this hard work don't blow it at the last hurdle and rob your friends of their yolk stroke moment, which they are all dying to post on Instagram. A short gentle warming to take the edge off and they are ready to finish and consume, no more than 1 minute.

When the yolk is just done, dollop the cod's roe on the bread without breaking the yolk, and sprinkle with Seaweed Powder and edible glitter. This bread doesn't like to sit around, so serve immediately and encourage your friends to dig in quick while you make the rest of the breads.

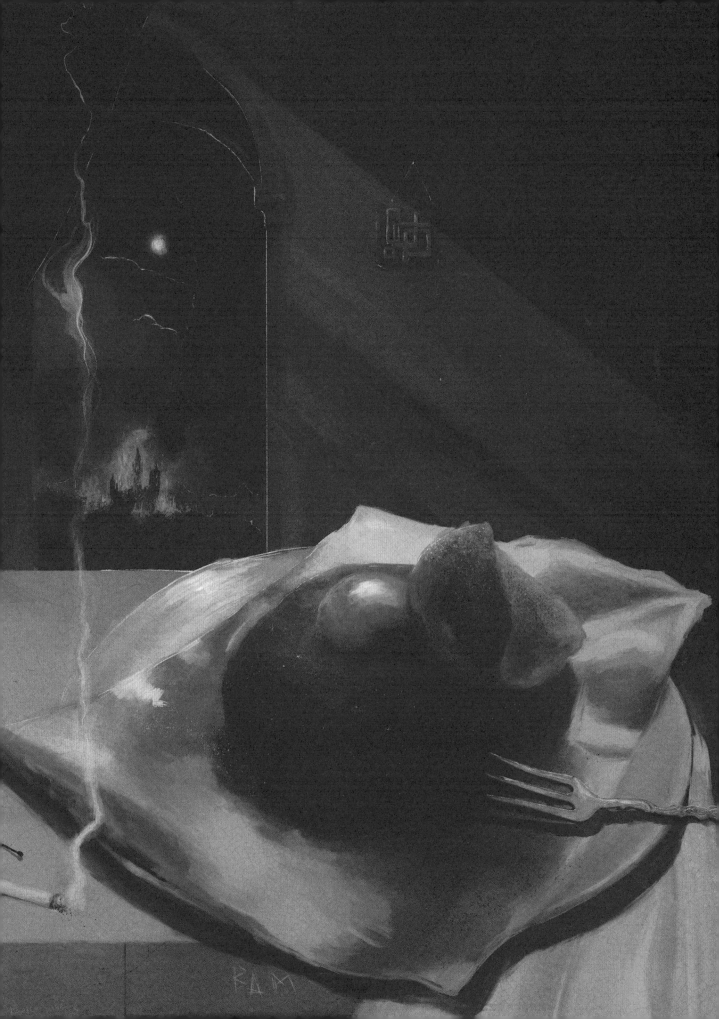

AUBERGINE AND RICOTTA FLATBREAD

This particular topping was born out of desperation, when squash was making its way out of season. We blister the aubergines (eggplant) in the oven then smoke them until they are on the verge of collapse. The onion and the garlic add depth, but we found this out by accident really – there were a lot of onions left over one night after service, so we added them to the aubergine rather than throw them away, and it somehow brought it to life. I like it when dishes come about like that.

ESSENTIAL EQUIPMENT
hand-held (immersion) blender
pizza oven, pizza stone or cast-iron frying pan (skillet)
(see pages 60–62)
2 pizza peels

MAKES 8
3 cloves garlic, peeled and sliced
2 tablespoons olive oil
1 medium onion, peeled and halved lengthways
sunflower oil
3 medium aubergines (eggplants)
30 ml (1 fl oz/2 tablespoons) pomegranate molasses
30 ml (1 fl oz/2 tablespoons) fermented turnip juice
(or water)
handful of nettle or mint leaves
butter, for frying
1 x quantity **BAM** Basic Flatbread Dough (page 58)
250 g/9 oz ricotta
red or black chilli flakes
Lemon Oil (page 198)
salt and freshly ground black pepper

Warm the olive oil in a frying pan (skillet) over medium heat and add the garlic. Cook for 5 minutes until soft and golden, then remove from the oil with a slotted spoon and set aside.

Preheat the oven to 200°C/400°F/Gas Mark 6. Toss the onion in a mixing bowl with a touch of sunflower oil and a generous pinch of salt. In a griddle pan over a high heat, blacken the cut side of the onion, around 3–4 minutes. Transfer to a baking sheet and roast in the oven until the onion has softened but still possess a little bite, around 20–25 minutes.

While the onion is roasting, blacken the aubergines (eggplants) in the griddle pan in the same way, turning occasionally until well charred. Transfer the aubergines to a separate baking sheet and roast in the oven until they soften and collapse, around 20 minutes. Lift them by their tops with tongs to remove from the baking sheet. The aubergines will be quite delicate, so have a plate or bowl handy to transfer them onto. Allow to cool for a few minutes so they can be handled easily. You can also cook the onion and aubergines on a barbecue, especially if you have used it to make your breads. Just blacken as above, and then move to a cooler part of the barbecue to fully soften.

To prepare the aubergines, pick the tops up and discard, then scoop out the flesh and transfer to a sieve over a bowl, pressing a little to get rid of any excess liquid. If there are a few bits of charred skin dotted through the aubergine don't worry too much, as it adds to the flavour. Tip the aubergines into a mixing bowl, and, using a hand-held (immersion) blender or food processor whizz with the pomegranate molasses, turnip juice or water, garlic and blackened onions to a smooth purée. Season to taste.

If you are using nettle leaves, heat a little butter in a frying pan (skillet) over a medium heat and fry a few at a time, until crisp. Season with salt then set aside on paper towels to soak up any excess fat. If you are using mint, keep it fresh.

Pat out the first piece of Flatbread Dough following the method on page 60. Once on the pizza peel, smear a heaped tablespoon or so of the aubergine and onion purée all over the dough with the back of a spoon. Follow the steps to cook the bread on pages 60–62. The dough should be blackened in places. Remove from the oven with the second pizza peel.

To serve, blob with the ricotta and sprinkle with the chilli flakes and nettles or mint. Finish with the Lemon Oil and a few grinds of black pepper. Repeat with the rest of the dough and toppings, and serve.

ST. JOHN RAREBIT

There are a few things I can't live without. St. JOHN Rarebit
is one of those things.

ESSENTIAL EQUIPMENT
heavy-based saucepan
pizza oven, pizza stone or cast-iron frying pan (skillet)
(see pages 60–62)
2 pizza peels

MAKES 10
2 tablespoons unsalted butter
2 tablespoons plain (all-purpose) flour
¼ teaspoon cayenne pepper
½ tablespoon mustard
1 tablespoon Worcestershire sauce, plus extra to serve
220 ml (7½ fl oz/scant 1 cup) Guinness
500 g (1 lb 2 oz/4 cups) strong Cheddar cheese, such as
Montgomery, grated
1 x quantity **BAM** Basic Flatbread Dough (page 58)

Select a saucepan with a heavy base that is big enough to
accommodate the ingredients, and has enough room to whisk
everything together vigorously. Place the saucepan over
a medium heat, add the butter and gently melt. Add the flour
and stir until it's incorporated and forms a roux. Continue
to cook for 2 minutes or so, stirring constantly. If it starts to
catch, turn the heat down. Add the cayenne and the mustard
to the pan and whisk in thoroughly.

Hit the pan with the Worcestershire sauce and whisk in
as best you can. Add a dribble of Guinness and incorporate,
then another splash of Guinness, then another, stirring the
whole time until it's fully mixed. Don't be tempted to rush this
step, because if you add the Guinness too quickly, it'll split.

Allow the mix to bubble for a minute or two, then start
adding handfuls of grated cheese, again stirring constantly
and incorporating each handful properly before adding the
next. When all the cheese has melted, pour the warm mix into
an airtight container. The rarebit mix will keep for a couple of
weeks in the refrigerator, but I doubt very much that it will be
hanging around that long.

Pat out the first piece of Flatbread Dough following the
method on page 60. Take a ball of rarebit mix, form it into a
circle and place on the dough so that it is covering the face of
the bread. Just under 1 cm (½ inch) thickness should do the
trick. Follow the steps to cook the bread on pages 60–62,
until it looks like bubbling toffee.

Make a series of grooves in the rarebit and douse generously
with Worcestershire sauce. Don't burn your mouth eating too
quickly. I find it very difficult to share rarebit and resent anyone
who just assumes I will share if I order or make one, so I advise
you serve one per person. And that's nothing to do with the fact
that I'm an only child.

LAMB OFFAL FLATBREAD

One of my all-time favourite things to eat is a freshly baked *lahmacun*, or Turkish pizza as it's sometimes known. Without sounding like a dickhead (which is usually a precursor to me sounding like one), however much I loved it, I always craved a bigger flavour. I thought, and still think, they could be better a lot of the time – they are never fully loaded, and the bread is pretty basic. I started wrapping adana-style kebabs in *lahmacun*, filling it with the zesty salad that often accompanies kebabs and with generous helpings of yogurt and chilli sauce. I had a fantasy flavour in my head that I couldn't quite find anywhere. Nailing that was largely the extent of my ambition when I opened **BAM**, and when I managed it, I felt like Gary and Wyatt in *Weird Science* when the closet door explodes and Lisa emerges ('So what would you little maniacs like to do first?'). It's the only dish to feature on every menu to date.

When we first started, I felt like I had to legitimize my food by making absolutely everything from scratch – I had a warped idea of gaining control of the uncontrollable, which faded after a while, but it was a valuable process to go through nonetheless. I bought in whole plucks of lamb offal from Farmer Tom, ten or twelve at a time, butchered each pluck, peeled the membrane off of every liver, deboned lamb breasts, picked the fat down, cut each piece of liver and heart into mincer-friendly pieces... you catch my drift. It's a pain to achieve in our kitchen with a semi-pro mincer, and even more difficult using most domestic mincing attachments – you end up with a kind of mulchy purée rather than a mince. Now we ask our supplier to mince the quantities we need for us, so I actually look forward to knocking the lamb offal up. I'm positive your local butcher will do the same for you if you ask them nicely and give them a few days' notice. Trust me, this recipe will be infinitely easier and much more fun if you get your butcher to mince (grind) everything for you. If you possess a mincer, have plenty of time, like mess and enjoy lots of washing up and sterilizing then by all means, mince the offal yourself. One thing you will have to do is poach and peel the lamb testicles, though. On more than one occasion while peeling the testicles for this recipe, I have been squirted in the face with ball juice that seeps into the membrane. It could just be my bad technique, but it would be rude of me if I didn't prepare you for that possibility.

ESSENTIAL EQUIPMENT
pizza oven, pizza stone or cast-iron frying pan (skillet)
(see pages 60–62)
2 pizza peels
digital thermometer

MAKES 8
6–8 lambs' testicles
500 g/1 lb 1¾ oz lambs' liver, minced (ground)
440 g/15 oz lamb heart, minced (ground)
440 g/15 oz lamb fat, minced (ground)
500 g/1 lb 1¾ oz lamb mince (ground lamb)
3½ tablespoons Bakken Spice (page 197)
200 g (7 oz/scant ¾ cup) *biber salcasi* (Turkish mild pepper paste)
1¼ tablespoons salt
1 x **BAM** Basic Flatbread Dough (page 58)
440 ml (15 fl oz/scant 2 cups) natural yogurt
1 x quantity Sumac Shallots (page 197)
1 medium bunch of flat leaf parsley, roughly chopped
chilli sauce, to serve

📷 P162/163

First, poach the lamb balls. This can be done a day or two before. Rinse and clean under cold water to remove any excess blood, then place in a saucepan and cover with about 2.5 cm (1 inch) water and season with salt. Bring to a boil, then simmer for 15–20 minutes, skimming off the froth that rises to the surface as you go. Test a testicle for tenderness by poking with a skewer – if it comes out with ease, they are done. Some may have popped but don't worry, it doesn't affect the end result. Cool under a running cold tap or place in an ice bath until they have chilled enough to handle. The edible part of the testicle resides within that thick, lemon-shaped membrane which needs to be removed and discarded. There shouldn't be too much resistance – just tear the membrane and work the inner sphere out. Carefully dry each testicle and dice into 1 cm (½ inch) pieces.

In a large mixing bowl, combine the liver, heart, fat and mince, using your hands to break up any clumps with your fingers (you might want to consider wearing disposable gloves). Add 425 ml (14½ fl oz/1¾ cups) water, Bakken Spice, *biber salçasi* and the salt and mix, then lastly, incorporate the testicles. The mix should be quite sloppy, which helps it to stick to the dough. If the mix is too dry, the topping will just tumble off the bread. You can use the mix straight away, or transfer to an airtight container, or into disposable piping (pastry) bags – which makes it easier and speedier to put the topping on when you are ready to cook the flatbreads – and chill until needed. It will keep for about 3 days.

If you are using a piping bag, snip 2 cm (¾ inch) off the tip. Pat out the first piece of Flatbread Dough following the method on page 60. Once on the pizza peel, pipe or spoon 3 lines of offal mix on to the dough, then lightly smear the offal over the dough with a spoon, leaving about 2.5 cm (1 inch) around the edge. The less force you can use, the less risk you run of ripping the bread.

There won't be a whole lot of browning on the offal, but the fat will cook it through and keep everything moist. If the temperature of your pizza oven is around 250–300°C/480–570°F then by the time your bread looks cooked, the meat will also be done. You can double check this by touching the meat with a probe – anything over 80°C/175°F is fine.

Remove from the oven with the second peel, then cut the bread into 8 slices using a pizza cutter or sharp knife before topping with the yogurt, chilli sauce, Sumac Shallots and parsley. Repeat with the rest of the dough and offal mixture and serve straight away.

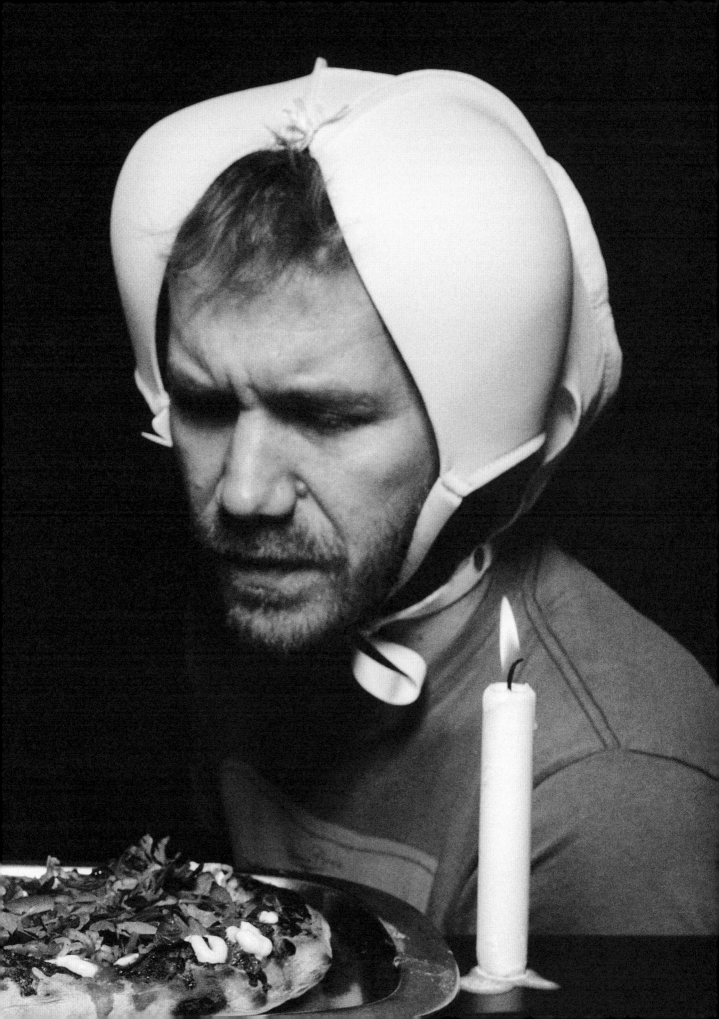

OXTAIL, BONE MARROW AND ANCHOVY

St. JOHN is one of the most influential restaurants on the planet. Championing ingredients such as heart, liver, brains, tripe and bone marrow, the nose-to-tail approach captured the imagination of chefs worldwide, reminding us all that the 'wobbly bits' are as delectable as the rest. A famous pearl of wisdom from Fergus is 'if you're going to kill an animal, it's only polite to eat the whole thing'. This is a homage to Fergus and St. JOHN.

Preheat the oven to 120°C/250°F/Gas Mark ½.

Toss the oxtail with the salt and saltpeter, if using, in a mixing bowl, along with the peeled garlic and thyme. Tip the oxtail, garlic and thyme into a casserole dish (Dutch oven) that snugly fits the meat, then pour over the IPA. Bear in mind that the beer or stout you use will punctuate the overall flavour of this dish, so choose something you like.

Cover the meat with a cartouche (a circle of baking/parchment paper) and then put a tightly fitting layer of aluminium foil over the dish; this will encourage the meat to steam, which retains its succulence. Cover with the lid, place on the middle shelf of the oven and cook for 4–6 hours. I've noticed some modern domestic ovens don't allow more than a few hours of continuous cooking, so double check your model for information. The oxtail should be a very rich, dark brown colour, and coming away from the bone with no effort at all.

Allow to cool to the point where you can handle it, then pick the meat and fat off the bone into a mixing bowl in as big pieces as you can. Discard the bones and strain the cooking liquid into a jug (pitcher). The liquid should be cool at this stage. You want the liquid to homogenize, and that's difficult if it's hot. Stir vigorously with a spoon or a small whisk and pour over the oxtail meat. Mix together gently and transfer the mixture into a (preferably) rectangular container, such as a 450 g/1 lb loaf pan. Wrap in clingfilm (plastic wrap) or cover with a lid and refrigerate until set, at least 6 hours, but preferably overnight. The longer you can leave it to set, the easier it will be to cut when the time comes. We set the oxtail in this shape so it can be cut somewhere close to the length and width of the bone marrow. Cut lengthways into 2.5-cm (1-inch) wide pieces with a very sharp knife. Rewrap and keep refrigerated until needed.

Next, make the parsley breadcrumbs. Blitz the breadcrumbs and the parsley together using a food processor or hand-held (immersion) blender in a deep mixing bowl, then chill in the refrigerator until needed.

ESSENTIAL EQUIPMENT
barbecue (see page 43)
casserole dish (Dutch oven)
450 g/1 lb loaf pan or other rectangular container
food processor or hand-held (immersion) blender

SERVES 4
8 pieces of 12.5 cm (5 inch) canoe-cut bone marrow
(ask your butcher to do this)
4 BAM Flatbreads (pages 56–63)

FOR THE OXTAIL
1 kg/2¼ oz fatty oxtail (preferably aged)
pinch of saltpeter (for colour; optional)
12 cloves garlic, peeled
sprig of thyme
330 ml (11 fl oz/generous 1¼ cups) IPA or stout
salt

FOR THE PARSLEY BREADCRUMBS
250 g (9 oz/5 cups) panko breadcrumbs
handful flat leaf parsley leaves

FOR THE SALAD
1 medium bunch flat leaf parsley, leaves picked
1 x quantity Anchovy Dressing (page 198)
Lemon Oil (page 198)
4 tablespoons Pickled Red Chillies (page 201)
4 tablespoons Pickled Red Onions (page 200)

Preheat the oven to 200°C/400°F/Gas Mark 6. Place the bones in a roasting pan and cook in the oven for 10–12 minutes – poke a skewer into the marrow, and if there's no resistance, they are done.

Once you're satisfied the bones are cooked, cover the surface of each bone with slices of oxtail and a sprinkling of breadcrumbs and switch the oven to the grill (broiler) setting. You don't need to cook the oxtail, just warm it through and crisp the crumb up a little, so grill (broil) for 3–4 minutes.

While the bones are finishing, get the parsley salad dressed. Toss the parsley with a generous drizzle of Anchovy Dressing and Lemon Oil then mix in the Pickled Red Chillies and Pickled Red Onions.

Arrange the bones on a serving platter with the salad. Revive the bread under the grill, cut into halves and stack next to the bones. Drizzle the rendered bone marrow fat from the bottom of the bone roasting pan over the bread and finish the bones with a scattering of sea salt flakes. Serve with a stack of napkins and crab picks or teaspoons to scoop the bone marrow and all its extras out onto the bread. Make sure you get a decent helping of the pickles with every bite. It's essential that you eat this with your hands.

MATTY MATHESON'S RETURN OF THE MAC

The two busiest and most fun nights in **BAM**'s history to date are the collaborative dinners we did with our brother **Matty**, who is humble, subtle and wise in equal measure. This tastes like a Big Mac 2.0, and I can't get enough of it. It's remarkably easy to recreate this at home.

ESSENTIAL EQUIPMENT
pizza oven, pizza stone or cast-iron frying pan (skillet)
(see pages 60–62)
2 pizza peels

MAKES 8
1 tablespoon beef dripping
600 g/1 lb 5 oz fatty minced (ground) beef (ask your butcher for aged beef if possible)
240 ml (8 fl oz/1 cup) chicken or beef stock (broth)
½ x quantity **BAM Basic Flatbread Dough** (page 58)
melted butter, for brushing
4 tablespoons sesame seeds
16 slices American cheese
400 g/1 lb firm mozzarella cheese, grated
1 x 340-g/12-oz jar gherkin (dill pickle) slices
1 onion, thinly sliced
large handful finely shredded iceberg lettuce
salt and freshly ground black pepper

FOR THE BURGER SAUCE
100 g (3½ oz/⅓ cup) French's mustard
4 tablespoons Heinz Ketchup
4 tablespoons Hellmann's Mayonnaise
1 tablespoon diced shallot
1 tablespoon diced gherkins

First, prepare the beef. Heat a frying pan (skillet) over a medium heat and melt the dripping in the pan, or if you can't get hold of any, use vegetable oil. Fry the minced (ground) beef, breaking up any big clumps, and season well with salt. When the beef has taken on a little colour, about 3–5 minutes, add the stock (broth). Simmer the beef gently for 15 minutes. Allow to cool. At this point, you can store it in an airtight container in the refrigerator to use later, or cook straight away.

To make the burger sauce, whisk all the ingredients together in a small bowl.

Pat out the first piece of Flatbread Dough following the method on page 60. Cover the perimeter of the bread with melted butter and scatter a liberal amount of sesame seeds over the butter.

Spoon some of the meat over the first pizza base; it's an idea to pat the meat down ever so gently, just to secure it to the dough, as this will stop you losing some of it when you transfer the bread to the oven.

Place the bread close to the flame in the oven. When one side of the bread starts to blister and colour, turn the bread 180 degrees and cook until golden and blistered on the other side, around 3–5 minutes.

Pull the bread to the mouth of the oven, place 2 slices of American cheese on the pizza and a smattering of grated mozzarella. Return to the oven to melt briefly – personally, I avoid any colouring of the cheese whatsoever. When the cheese has melted, retrieve the pizza from the oven. Apply lashings of burger sauce and gherkin (dill pickle) slices and a smattering of sliced white onion. Finish with a pile of iceberg lettuce. Repeat with the rest of the dough and ingredients.

I fold this pizza in half and eat in one sitting, oblivious to anyone else in my presence, but you can be polite and cut it into slices to share round while you are waiting for the rest of the pizzas to cook, if you are of a generous nature. Have lots of paper napkins ready to wipe burger sauce from your chin.

SWEET

AFTER DINNER MINT ICE CREAM

The Jägermeister in this recipe can be switched for whatever digestif you prefer. I've made this with Gammel Dansk, Fernet Branca and Underberg. Three good things that follow a meal – ice cream, a digestif and After Eight mint chocolates – are crystallized in one perfect mouthful.

ESSENTIAL EQUIPMENT
digital thermometer
fine mesh sieve
ice cream machine

SERVES 10
750 ml (25 fl oz/3 cups) whole (full-fat) milk
375 ml (12½ fl oz/1½ cups) double (heavy) cream
10 egg yolks
150 g (5 oz/¾ cup) caster (superfine) sugar
350 ml (12 fl oz/1½ cups) Jägermeister
8 After Eight mints, finely chopped

FOR THE CHOCOLATE SHELL COATING
2 tablespoons vegetable oil
225 g/8 oz 70% cocoa solids dark chocolate, broken into pieces
1 tablespoon sea salt flakes

TO SERVE
60 g/2 oz Mint Aero or Mint Matchmakers, or both if you're feeling particularly enthusiastic, roughly chopped

 P174

First, make the chocolate shell coating. Warm the oil and the chocolate in a small saucepan over a low heat. Whisk the oil and the chocolate together until incorporated, then take off the heat and allow to cool. Mix in the salt and store in an airtight container at room temperature until ready to use. This will keep for 3 days or so.

To make the ice cream, pour the milk and cream into a saucepan and bring to the boil, then remove from the heat.

In a large mixing bowl, whisk together the egg yolks and sugar, then pour the milk and cream mixture over the eggs in a steady stream, whisking until incorporated. Tip the mix into a clean saucepan and return to a very low heat. If the mix cooks too much and splits, you will have to start again, so please don't rush this stage by trying to speed up the process and thickening over a high heat. Stir gently with a spatula constantly until the mixture reaches 80–82°C/176–180°F, or it coats the spatula and is a custard-like consistency.

Strain though a fine mesh sieve, then add the Jägermeister and stir well. Chill in the refrigerator (ideally overnight), then churn in an ice cream machine following the manufacturer's instructions. Once churned, scoop out of the machine and fold in the chopped After Eights, then spoon into a plastic airtight container and return to the freezer.

To serve, warm the chocolate shell coating in a small saucepan over a low heat, until it's just pourable. Scoop the ice cream into balls and arrange in individual bowls. Pour over the chocolate shell coating, and sprinkle over the chopped Mint Aero or Mint Matchmakers before the coating sets.

WHISKEY AND HONEY ICE CREAM

It took a while to convince me to put a dessert on the menu, but this worked well for us when the restaurant got crazy busy, as front of house could just run down and grab them from the freezer. We served it in disposable espresso cups with the coffee crumb on top. This also goes well with the Banana and Cinnamon Flatbread (page 80).

ESSENTIAL EQUIPMENT
electric whisk or stand mixer

SERVES 10
3 eggs
100 g (3½ oz/½ cup) demerara sugar
75 g (2⅔ oz/scant ¼ cup) honey
450 ml (15 fl oz/scant 2 cups) double (heavy) cream
150 ml (5 fl oz/⅔ cup) Jameson or other Irish whiskey

FOR THE COFFEE CRUMB
1½ teaspoons instant coffee granules
65 g (2½ oz/¾ stick) unsalted butter, at room temperature, plus extra for greasing
65 g (2½ oz/⅓ cup) muscovado or brown sugar
1½ tablespoons caster (superfine) sugar
2 tablespoons unsweetened cocoa powder
2 tablespoons plain (all-purpose) flour
pinch of sea salt flakes

In a mixing bowl with an electric whisk or in a stand mixer with the whisk attachment, mix the eggs, sugar and honey until thick; 8–10 minutes should do it. The eggs need to get to a point where they won't thicken any more.

In a separate bowl, whip the cream to firm peaks, then fold in the whiskey. The whiskey will loosen the cream a touch. Using a spatula, tip the cream into the bowl with the eggs and combine by very gently, folding the two together. Spoon the mix into a large, family-style serving bowl (or spoon into individual bowls), then wrap in a tight layer of cling film (plastic wrap) and freeze for at least 8 hours, preferably overnight.

While the mix is freezing, make the crumb. Dissolve the coffee in 1 teaspoon of boiling water and allow to cool. In a stand mixer or bowl, mix the butter with the sugars, cocoa powder, flour and salt until fully incorporated. Stir in the coffee, then chill in the refrigerator for 15 minutes.

Preheat the oven to 160ºC/325ºF/Gas Mark 3.

Line a baking sheet with baking (parchment) paper secured with a little butter. Using your fingers, crumble the crumb mix evenly in one layer onto the baking sheet and bake for 8–10 minutes. Inspect the crumb, mix it up and bake in the oven for a further 5 minutes, or until the mix starts to crisp up. Allow to cool. If not using straight away, you can store it in an airtight container for up to 1 week in the refrigerator.

When you are ready to eat, take the dish or dishes out of the freezer before you want to serve, and scatter the crumb over the top just before it goes to the table. It's a nice touch to heat the crumb in the oven for a few moments just to warm it slightly, but it's not essential.

RHUBARB AND TEQUILA GRANITA

This cleanses the palate beautifully before or after a meal.

Toss the sugar and the rhubarb together in a mixing bowl with 100 ml (3½ fl oz/scant ½ cup) water, then tip into a roasting pan and leave to macerate for 1 hour. The sugar will extract the juice from the rhubarb.

Preheat the oven to 180ºC/350ºF/Gas Mark 4.

Place the roasting pan of rhubarb in the oven and cook until tender but not burnt, around 7–8 minutes. Allow to cool completely then spoon into a food processor with a pinch of salt and whizz to a purée.

Pour the purée into a plastic container, add the lime juice and zest, and the tequila. Place somewhere flat in the freezer and freeze, uncovered, for 2–3 hours, scraping with a fork every hour or so until it looks like a Slush Puppie.

Scoop into small bowls or glasses and serve with a little extra tequila on top and a sprinkling of lime zest.

ESSENTIAL EQUIPMENT
food processor

SERVES 6-8
200 g (7 oz/1 cup) caster (superfine) sugar
500 g/1 lb 2 oz rhubarb, washed and roughly chopped
juice of 2 limes and zest of 1, plus extra zest to serve
75 ml (2½ fl oz/⅓ cup) tequila, plus extra to serve
salt

📷 P175

PEANUT AND FOIE GRAS BAR WITH C__T BISCUITS

The creation of these ice cream bars was an evolutionary process. I was in a small ice cream parlour that I always visit with my family in Brantôme, France, when I first saw foie gras ice cream. It is the only ice cream that they won't let you sample during the agonizing process of choosing which flavour combination to go for. The deliberation begins way before we reach the shop. The fear of making a poor choice is real, especially for the kids, and Kate wrestles with **FOMO** at the best of times, so trying to make a decision with **50**-plus ice creams with a multitude of flavour combos can become stressful. We limit ourselves to **2** scoops... and no bright blue bubble gum flavours, or whatever 'Smurf' flavour is, are allowed, and crucially, we all understand and agree that we don't share. I usually go for one scoop lemon sorbet, one scoop cassis. On this occasion though, I went for popcorn ice cream and a ball of foie gras. The stress over the decision to get a whole scoop of ice cream I couldn't sample was unjustified. The combo was ok, but they were both pretty rich – I'd chosen badly. So next time I picked something tart to cut through the fat of the foie gras – which ended up being cherry ice cream. Foie gras and cherry is a classic combination, and I've always been a sucker for the ricotta and cherry gelato (and every other flavour) from Gelupo in Soho, London.

The foie gras ice cream, I felt, still lacked conviction – it somehow tasted more like butter. But I loved the idea, and unashamedly stole it after some advice from Kitty Travers of La Grotta Ices. I put the **BAM** version of foie gras ice cream into a doughnut with Luxardo cherries.

Organisation is key to the success of this recipe so get everything you need in place before embarking on each step. I've included both a Thermomix method and domestic appliance method for the ice cream, as both warrant a place in this recipe.

A note on proportions: the white chocolate magic shell makes more than needed, but it's essential to have surplus to make sure the bars are fully coated, and it can be reused – I like to jazz up a scoop of dark chocolate ice cream with it from time to time. In addition, this makes six more peanut butter centres than needed because it's impossible to make in a smaller quantity, but they can easily be eaten as they are, perhaps with a black coffee to balance the sweetness.

We first made these biscuits for our annual Burn's Night extravaganza at Quo Vadis in Soho, London. They are delicious just rolled out on their own without a profanity embossed into them, but a cookie cutter is essential. There are various letter and number stamps available on the **World Wide Web** for you to choose, along with cookie cutters, and we got the lot for less than **£10 ($12)**. Kate and I love the word 'cunt', and the reaction it can receive. To be honest, our most common usage of it is as a powerful compliment. Personally, we would rather be called **CUNT** than **NICE** any day of the week.

ESSENTIAL EQUIPMENT
hand-held (immersion) blender
1 x Silikomart Silicone mould No 9
1 x Silikomart Silicone mould No 30
1 x reliable, recently calibrated digital thermometer
Thermomix (optional)

MAKES 9 BARS

FOR THE PEANUT BUTTER CENTRES (MAKES 15)
60 g (2¼ oz/¼ cup) caster (superfine) sugar
75 ml (2½ fl oz/⅓ cup) whole (full-fat) milk
75 ml (2½ fl oz/⅓ cup) double (heavy) cream
2 egg yolks
1 tablespoon peanut butter
pinch of salt

FOR THE FOIE GRAS ICE CREAM
50 g/2 oz egg yolk
55 g (2 oz/¼ cup) caster (superfine) sugar
75 ml (2½ fl oz/⅓ cup) whole (full-fat) milk
150 g/5 oz fresh, first-grade foie gras, diced
1 gelatine sheet, soaked
pinch of salt
200 ml (7 fl oz/scant 1 cup) double (heavy) cream

FOR THE CHERRY GEL
500 g (1 lb 2 oz) sour black cherry purée
½ teaspoon agar agar

FOR THE WHITE CHOCOLATE MAGIC SHELL
300 g/10½ oz white chocolate chips, melted
100 g/3⅓ oz raw coconut oil, melted
pinch of salt

TO SERVE
multicoloured sprinkles

📷 P179

TO MAKE THE PEANUT BUTTER CENTRES

I strongly advise that you make these at least 24 hours in advance of making the ice cream. Tip the sugar into a dry frying pan (skillet) over a medium-high heat and allow to melt without stirring, 4–5 minutes. I tend not to cook caramels on the highest heat as the sugar can caramelize quite quickly, and if the heat is too aggressive it can burn, especially in smaller quantities. When the caramel is a shade lighter than a cup of black coffee, add the milk and cream. This will bubble and spit, so exercise caution. Reduce the heat to low and simmer until the caramel has dissolved completely. Blend the yolks, peanut butter and salt in a small bowl with a hand-held (immersion) blender. Pour the hot caramel over the yolk and peanut butter mix. Blend until smooth, then allow to cool. Pour into the No 9 moulds, filling the cavities, then freeze.

Before you start mixing the ice cream base, pop the frozen peanut butter centres out of their moulds. Arrange on a tray and return to the freezer.

THERMOMIX ICE CREAM METHOD

Put the egg yolks, sugar and milk into the Thermomix. Set on 6, and the temperature to 80°C/175°F and blend. When it hits this temperature, it should have thickened. Continue to spin, adding the foie gras a little at a time. The temperature will drop slightly with the addition of the foie. Keep spinning until the temperature reaches 70°C/160°F. Add the soaked gelatine and a pinch of salt. Continue to spin for 1 minute without the heat setting.

SAUCEPAN ICE CREAM METHOD

For those not blessed with a Thermomix, this method works well still, there's just a bit more of a process involved. Whisk the yolks and sugar together in a mixing bowl. Bring the milk to a boil in a saucepan, remove from the heat and add to the eggs and sugar, exactly like a conventional custard. Return the mix back to the pan and cook over a low heat, continually stirring and scraping the base of the pan with a spatula until it hits 80°C/175°F. A digital thermometer is essential for an accurate reading. Pour the mix into a blender. Add the foie and blend on the highest setting until homogenized. Add this back to the pan, cooking like custard again, until the thermometer reads 70°C/160°F. Whisk in the gelatine and salt.

Pass the mixture through a fine sieve in to a large bowl set in iced water. Stir the mix until chilled.

When the foie mix is cold, whip the cream to soft peaks, and fold into the chilled foie mix until fully incorporated.

Fill the No 30 moulds three quarters of the way to the top – the idea is to suspend the peanut butter centres in the middle of the bar surrounded by the foie ice cream. Place one peanut butter centre in the middle of the moulds. Top up each bar with the remaining ice cream mixture. Level off with a palette knife then freeze flat for 24 hours.

Next, make the cherry gel. Bring the purée to a simmer in a small saucepan and add the agar agar. Cook over a low heat for 5 minutes. Pass through a sieve then chill in the refrigerator until set. Once cold, blitz for 5 minutes on the highest setting of your blender and set aside.

To make the magic shell, whisk the melted chocolate and oil together with a pinch of salt and allow to cool to room temperature.

Now you are ready to coat the ice cream bars. Have the sprinkles ready in a shallow bowl. Pop the bars out of the moulds onto a cooling rack in a shallow roasting pan. Transfer the magic shell into a jug (pitcher) and pour over one bar, until fully coated, then scatter over the sprinkles – the shell starts to freeze almost instantly so you have a small window of opportunity for them to adhere. Repeat with the rest of the bars and then refreeze until ready to serve.

When ready to eat, remove the bars from the freezer and hold at room temperature for 8–10 minutes. Spoon a generous amount of cherry gel onto individual serving plates. Place the bar on top of the gel and serve with a C__t Biscuit (see overleaf). →

TO MAKE THE C__T BISCUITS

In a stand mixer, cream the butter and sugar together. When well mixed, beat in the egg. Stop the mixer, add the flour, baking powder, coconut and lime zest. Mix at a low speed until fully incorporated.

Form the dough into a rough square or rectangle on a floured work surface, if you can, as you want to roll the dough out into a squareish shape when it comes to cutting them out. Wrap the dough in cling film (plastic wrap) and chill for an hour or so. This will firm up the dough making it easier to roll out.

While the dough is chilling, preheat the oven to 180°C/350°F/ Gas Mark 4.

Line a couple of baking sheets with baking (parchment) paper. Retrieve the biscuit (cookie) dough from the refrigerator, lightly flour the work surface and roll into an even rectangle or square to about 5 mm (¼ inch) thick. Mine are 8.5 × 13 cm (3⅓ × 5 inches). Place the cutter as close to the edge as possible, maximizing the amount of biscuits (cookies) you will get out of the square. Press the cutter down firmly, release and wriggle free. Stamp in your chosen word, make sure it's bold and readable, then you're good to go. Cut the rest of the biscuits out and stamp with the letters, transfer them to the baking sheet and cook until golden, around 10 minutes. If your oven is like mine and gets hotter at the back, turn the baking sheets around half way through the cooking time to achieve an even colour.

Finish with a light sprinkling of golden caster sugar around the edges while they are hot from the oven, being careful not to obscure the lettering.

Allow to cool on a wire rack and then serve with the Peanut and Foie Gras Bar (see previous page) or store in an airtight container and eat as they are. They should keep well for 4–5 days.

ESSENTIAL EQUIPMENT
stand mixer
cookie cutter
letter stamp

MAKES ABOUT 20
100 g (3½ oz/¾ stick plus 1 tablespoon) butter, softened
100 g (3½ oz/½ cup) golden caster (superfine) sugar, plus extra for dusting
1 large egg, beaten
200 g (7 oz/1¾ cups) plain (all-purpose) flour
¼ teaspoon baking powder
60 g (2¼ oz/⅔ cup) desiccated (shredded) coconut
zest of ¼ lime
pinch of sea salt flakes

'Cunt' is related to words from India, China, Ireland, Rome and Egypt. Such words were either titles of respect for women, priestesses and witches, or derivatives of the names of various goddesses. In ancient writings, the word 'cunt' was synonymous with 'woman' though not in the insulting modern sense. (Barbara G. Walker, 1983)

Negative reactions to 'cunt' resonate from a learned fear of ancient yet contemporary, inherent yet lost, reviled yet redemptive 'cunt-power'. (Inga Muscio, 2002)

DEEP-FRIED MINCE PIE

Celebrate the excessive Christmas season with a 1000-calorie deep-fried mince pie. We do a deep-fried cherry pie at **BAM**, which was introduced by chef Ravneet Gill. If you want to make the cherry version at home, swap out the mince pie filling for canned cherries. You can fill these with any kind of purée. While not an attractive name, the slurry is essential to the success of this recipe.

I've always loved making biscuits (cookies), cakes and bread with my kids. It creates a huge mess which isn't so much fun to clear up but home baking is a lot of fun and a rewarding way to spend rainy afternoons when you can't have a kick about outside. Soda bread is our current favourite thing to make. There is no creaming of butter and sugar in tabletop mixers for tiny three-year-old fingers to get trapped in, it's just a case of weighing everything out, mixing and baking. Every time I've attempted anything too ambitious with the kids it's turned out wrong which is unfair on the kids as the best bit for them is a sweet treat at the end as a reward for their time and effort. That's why I'm recommending shop-bought puff pastry for this recipe. We make ours at **BAM** but it's a reasonably long process and I have never attempted to make puff pastry at home so I'm not including one here. When I asked each of my chefs, they too have never attempted to make puff at home either. If you're that keen, there are straightforward recipes with video guides online.

ESSENTIAL EQUIPMENT
food processor
deep-fat fryer

SERVES 8
375 g/13¼ oz shop-bought puff pastry
320 g/11¼ oz mince pie filling
1 egg, beaten
200 g (7 oz/1¾ cups) plain (all-purpose) flour
350 ml sparkling water
100 ml (3½ fl oz/scant ½ cup) neutral oil
10 g/¼ oz salt
sunflower or vegetable oil, for deep frying

TO SERVE
icing (confectioners') sugar
clotted cream or ice cream
zest of 1 orange

Roll out the pastry on a chopping (cutting) board and cut it into 8 equal rectangles. Spoon an eighth of the mince pie filling onto half of one of the puff pastry rectangles. Brush the outer edge of the pastry with the beaten egg. Fold over the vacant edge. Press down the two sides and crimp along the edge with a fork. Repeat with the other 7 pies. Place the pies on a tray, cover and place in the freezer until completely frozen.

Next make the slurry. Add the flour, sparkling water, oil and salt to a food processor or the cup of a hand-held (immersion) blender) and blend everything together. Once fully combined, pour into a bowl.

Preheat the oven to 110°C/225°F/Gas Mark ¼. Heat the oil in the deep-fat fryer to 160°C/325°F.

Retrieve a pie from the freezer, dunk it in the slurry and gently lay it in the deep-fat fryer. I can get 2 pies in my fryer at home. Cook for 7–8 minutes, until golden brown and crisp. When cooked, drain on kitchen paper. Transfer the fried pies to a roasting pan fitted with a wire rack and place in the oven while you repeat the process with the remaining pies.

Dust with icing (confectioners') sugar and serve with clotted cream or ice cream and the zest of an orange.

A NOTE ON
BAM COCKTAILS

RYAN CHETIYAWARDANA, AKA MR LYAN

When we met with Lee and Kate, it was obvious to us that cocktails would be a great fit for BAM. Not only would it allow for some bold flavours to bounce off the food (I'd had the pleasure of sampling the cooking early when my partner Anette invited Lee to cook at her roastery), but also to match the fun of what they planned for the restaurant. A big side was the practicality, too. We wanted drinks that packed a punch, but were super quick to serve. With this in mind, and with Lee's love of Jameson noted, we created the BAM Whiskey Sourz with an extra layer of bright acidity that would cut through some of the bigger dishes. Included here is an adapted version, along with a super fun mash-up between a Lagerita and a Chelada that is also great with richer dishes.

DRINKS

GIN AND TONIC SLUSHIE

This is hard to rush. Putting everything together is easy peasy, but you're limited to the performance of your freezer, so I generally make this a least a day in advance to be safe. I feel this makes watching tennis way more fun.

Warm 100 ml (3½ fl oz/scant ½ cup) water in a saucepan over a low heat, add the sugar and allow to dissolve. Take off the heat to cool a little and mix in the gin, juices and tonic water. Transfer the liquid to a shallow container suitable for freezing. Freeze for at least 2 hours.

After 2 hours, give the solution a stir and a scrape with a fork and return to the freezer. Repeat this every hour or so until the liquid is all slushy.

Before serving, scrape and mix back to a slush consistency. Spoon into chilled glasses and drink through a wide straw.

ESSENTIAL EQUIPMENT
shallow, freezer-proof container
wide straws

SERVES 8-10
190 g (6¾ oz/scant 1 cup) caster (superfine) sugar
250 ml (8 fl oz/1 cup) gin
juice of 1 lemon
juice of 1 lime
500 ml (17 fl oz/generous 2 cups) tonic water

📷 P190

LE LAGERITA

We use our favourite stubbies of French lager for this (Coors Banquet is a good substitute, but any light lager will work grand), and spike it with some tequila for added fun times. When it's hot, the salinity is great, but it also makes it a good choice with food.

First, make the hibiscus honey water. Add the hibiscus flowers and orange peel to 200 ml (7 fl oz/scant 1 cup) boiling water. Allow to cool a little, then stir in the honey. Make sure it's well mixed, then strain out the peel and flowers. Keep in a clean, airtight container in the refrigerator until needed. This will make enough for plenty of drinks.

To make the thyme salt, pulse the salt, lemon thyme and vanilla in a food processor, then store in an airtight container until needed.

Wet the rim of a highball with the lime, then dunk it in the thyme salt. Make sure none is in the glass, and wipe the inside of the rim to remove any excess. Using a potato peeler, take a long strip of cucumber, and fancily wrap it around the inside of the glass and fill with cubed ice. Squeeze the remainder of the lime in, then add the other ingredients, stir, add more ice and top with lager.

ESSENTIAL EQUIPMENT
food processor

MAKES 1
½ lime
Thyme Salt (see below)
1 cucumber
35 ml/1¼ fl oz 100% agave tequila
15 ml/½ fl oz Hibiscus Honey Water (see below)
hot sauce (optional)
250 ml/8 fl oz bottle light French lager

FOR THE THYME SALT
100 g/3½ oz sea salt flakes
5 sprigs lemon thyme
seeds from ¼ vanilla pod

FOR THE HIBISCUS HONEY WATER
1 teaspoon dried hibiscus flowers
1 strip orange peel
250 ml (8 fl oz/1 generous cup) honey

📷 P191

SUPER LYAN X BAM
WHISKEY SOURZ

ESSENTIAL EQUIPMENT
muslin (cheesecloth)
blender

SERVES 1
1 egg white (don't be put off, this is just to give
a nice richness)
60 ml (2 fl oz/¼ cup) Jameson whiskey
20 ml/¾ fl oz lemon juice
20 ml/¾ fl oz raspberry anise shrub (see below)

FOR THE RASPBERRY-ANISE SHRUB
150 g/5 oz raspberries
1 star anise
350 ml (12 fl oz/1½ cups) cider vinegar
500 g (1 lb 2 oz/2½ cups) golden caster
(superfine) sugar

📷 P192

A different version to the one in the restaurant, but hassle free (just do the shrub ahead of time; it'll keep for **3** weeks in the refrigerator). Simply blitz up for one or many.

First, make the shrub. Tip the raspberries, anise and cider vinegar into a bowl and leave to infuse for 2–3 hours.

Pour the mix into a saucepan and bring to a gentle boil. Cook over a medium heat on a rolling boil for 10 minutes, then remove from the heat and add the sugar. Stir to dissolve, allow to cool, then strain through a sieve lined with muslin (cheesecloth). Pour into a clean bottle and chill until needed.

Pour the egg white into a blender with a couple of ice cubes. Add all the other ingredients then blend until chilled and strain over more ice into a rocks glass to serve.

PICKLEBACK

This is my favourite cocktail of all time. I had my first Pickleback in New York City in 2009. Where exactly? I can't remember... God Bless America. You will need a juicer of some description to juice the cucumber, and some muslin (cheesecloth) or jelly-making bag set up kinda thing, a few friends, and an abundance of shot glasses. Never use a peated whiskey for this, and limit yourself to five or six, tops.

In a large lidded saucepan, warm the vinegar over a medium heat and dissolve the sugar into it. Toss in all the other ingredients for the pickle juice except the cucumber, cover and simmer on the lowest heat possible for 2 hours. Allow to cool. Strain the vinegar through a sieve lined with muslin (cheesecloth) into a clean bowl or jug. Squeeze every drop out of the ingredients in the muslin to extract all the juice and flavour. This should give you about 400 ml (14 fl oz/1⅔ cups) spicy vinegar.

Juice the cucumbers until you have roughly 600 ml (20 fl oz/2½ cups). Combine with the spicy vinegar, funnel into a bottle and chill.

Once chilled, line up the shot glasses, two per person, and a round of beers. Fill one glass with whiskey and the other with the pickle juice. Shoot the whiskey, then the pickle juice, then shoot the beer.

ESSENTIAL EQUIPMENT
muslin (cheesecloth)
juicer

MAKES 1 LITRE (34 FL OZ/4 CUPS)

FOR THE PICKLE JUICE
500 ml (17 fl oz/2 cups) rice wine vinegar
or white wine vinegar
200 g (7 oz/scant 1 cup) palm or demerara sugar
4 long red chillies, finely chopped
4 bird's eye chillies, finely chopped
60 g/2 oz galangal, grated
3 lemongrass stalks, chopped
200 g/7 oz ginger, grated
100 g/3½ oz fresh turmeric, grated
8 cloves garlic, minced
8 kaffir lime leaves
6 cucumbers

TO SERVE
Jameson whiskey
American lager, ice cold

📷 P193

BAM BASICS

BAM DOUGHNUTS

You will need to start this recipe a day before you want to eat the doughnuts, to allow the dough to rest in the refrigerator overnight. When it comes to cooking the doughnuts, it's advisable to have everything organized. This will absolutely minimize the stress... remember cooking at home for friends should be fun so make life easy for yourself.

ESSENTIAL EQUIPMENT

stand mixer
deep-fat fryer

MAKES 10

2 eggs
zest of 1 orange
8 g/$\frac{1}{3}$ oz fresh yeast or 1 teaspoon dried active yeast
2 tablespoons caster (superfine) sugar
5 g ($\frac{1}{4}$ oz/1 teaspoon) fine salt
250 g (9 oz/2$\frac{1}{3}$ cups) strong flour, plus extra for dusting
65 g (2$\frac{1}{2}$ oz/$\frac{3}{4}$ stick) butter, softened
vegetable oil, for deep frying

FOR THE COATING

200 g (7 oz/1 cup) caster (superfine) sugar
2 tablespoons cinnamon

In the bowl of a stand mixer, add 75 ml (2$\frac{1}{2}$ fl oz/$\frac{1}{3}$ cup) water followed by the eggs, zest, yeast, sugar, salt and flour. Use the paddle attachment to mix on a medium speed for 6–7 minutes, until the dough comes completely away from the bowl, then allow to rest for 2–3 minutes.

When rested, turn the mixer back to medium speed and slowly add the butter a little lump at a time, until fully incorporated. Increase the speed as high as your machine will comfortably handle – my one does an R2 D2 impression and threatens to leap off the kitchen counter. The dough should form back into a ball after 5 minutes or so. Stop the mixer at this point. By now the mixture should be super silky, ultra-stretchy and warm to the touch.

Remove the paddle, cover the top of the bowl tightly with cling film (plastic wrap) and prove the dough in a warm place until doubled in size, around 1 hour. When ready, unwrap the bowl and knock back the dough. Place in a plastic container with a tight-fitting lid and place the dough in the refrigerator overnight.

Cut ten 10 cm (4 inch) squares of baking (parchment) paper.

An hour or so before you want to cook the doughnuts, spread the baking paper squares on a tray or trays deep enough to be wrapped in cling film when proving. Remove the dough from the refrigerator and portion into 50 g (2 oz) lumps.

Lightly dust the work surface with flour, then take a lump of dough and cup your hand over it. Using the work surface and your cupped hand, manipulate the dough into a smooth ball. Do your best not to get the dough too warm as it becomes hard to manage. Place the ball on the baking paper square. The baking paper prevents the dough sticking to the tray while proving. Once all the doughnuts are rolled, wrap the tray in cling film while you prepare the fryer and coating.

Before you start cooking, mix the sugar and cinnamon in a medium bowl, ready to toss the doughnuts in when they come out of the fryer. Have a tray lined with paper towels and have a tray with a wire rack waiting to rest the doughnuts on. Follow the maximum oil level guide recommended by the manufacturer of the deep-fat fryer and heat to 180°C/350°F.

Use the baking paper to lift the first doughnut out of the tray. Pull the paper with the doughnut onto a slotted spoon, then drop the doughnut, paper and all, into the fryer. Hit the start button on the timer. The paper will fall off the doughnut eventually. Use your tongs to lift out the paper and shake the oil off the paper over the fryer. After 2 minutes, flip the doughnut and cook for a further 2 minutes. Lift the cooked doughnut out and place on the plate lined with the paper to soak up a little of that excess oil. Repeat with the rest of the doughnuts, then toss them into the cinnamon sugar until completely coated. Set aside on a wire rack to cool.

SMOKED POTATOES AND JERUSALEM ARTICHOKES

It might seem excessive to fire up a barbecue to smoke 150 g (5 oz) potatoes for flatbread, which is why I left it optional in the Flatbread recipe (page 58). If you do choose to do it, though, I would suggest smoking 1 kg (2$\frac{1}{4}$ lb) and using them up over a couple of weeks, as they keep well in the refrigerator, and you can also roast them in a little oil to serve as a side. When I do this at home, I smoke them over a dying barbecue that I've just finished cooking on. I used Jerusalem artichokes (sunchokes) in the bread in Copenhagen, where BAM started in 2014. The earthy, mineral flavour complimented the smoke beautifully, as well as the sour notes in the bread itself. They are more expensive and seasonal, but I would argue that they make a more interesting bread.

ESSENTIAL EQUIPMENT

barbecue (see page 43)
oak, cherry or chestnut wood

MAKES 1 KG (2$\frac{1}{4}$ OZ)

1 kg (2$\frac{1}{4}$ lb) new potatoes or Jerusalem artichokes (sunchokes), scrubbed
2 tablespoons salt

Boil the new potatoes or Jerusalem artichokes in a large saucepan of water with a good handful of salt for 8–10 minutes, or until tender. Drain and allow to cool.

When cold enough to handle, squash the potatoes between the palms of your hands, breaking the skin slightly and exposing the potato within.

Set up your barbecue following the off-set method (see page 43) and allow to slowly burn down. When the coal is at a low heat, add two chunks of soaked hardwood such as oak, cherry or chestnut to the coal pile. Soaking the wood stops it from catching straight away, but if you've got bigger pieces of wood it's not essential. The coals shouldn't be hot enough to ignite the wood anyway, and what you're looking for is a slow smoulder that encourages smoke to flavour the already cooked potatoes.

Place the rack on the barbecue with the potatoes over the space that is devoid of coals. Put the lid on with the vent open a touch to draw the smoke through the spuds. It's important to monitor the potatoes, but if you keep taking the lid off they will never smoke. It's safe to leave them be for at least 30 minutes. The spuds are done when they have turned a pleasing golden colour.

Allow to cool and refrigerate in an airtight container. They must be cold before being introduced to the dough.

BUTTERMILK-FRIED SHALLOT RINGS

MAKES 100 G (3½ OZ/1 CUP)

2 large banana shallots, peeled and cut
into 1 cm (½ inch) rounds
250 ml (8 fl oz/1 cup) buttermilk, thin yogurt or milk
vegetable oil, for frying
flour, for dredging
salt

Separate out the shallot slices to individual rings. Tip into a bowl, sprinkle with a pinch of salt and cover with the buttermilk.

Get a pan hot with a good 2.5 cm (1 inch) oil in it. In a small shallow bowl, scatter a handful of flour and use to dredge the shallot rings. Shake off the excess and fry until golden and crispy, 3–4 minutes. Drain on kitchen paper. Season with salt again while hot.

SUMAC SHALLOTS

MAKES 100 G (3½ OZ/1½ CUPS)

3 banana shallots, peeled
1 teaspoon sumac
juice of ½ lemon
salt

Using a sharp knife or a mandoline to avoid bruising the shallots, which can make them bitter, thinly slice them into rings. Mix with the sumac and a squeeze of lemon and season with a pinch of salt. This can be done the day before serving and stored in an airtight container in the refrigerator, though the more in advance you do it, the less crunchy the shallots will be.

SEAWEED POWDER

Nori sheets are the most reliable and readily available seaweed you can use to make this. They also powder well. We use dried wakame to enhance the colour, but any seaweed that has good flavour will work handsomely.

ESSENTIAL EQUIPMENT

mini food processor

MAKES 10 G/½ OZ

5 sheets nori

In a mini food processor, blitz the nori to a fine powder, or as fine as it will go. Pop it into an airtight container and keep in a dry place until needed. It lasts forever, so if you've made a ton it's cool. Next time you're making a lamb stew or fish broth add a tablespoon or two for a boost of umami.

BAKKEN SPICE

Bakken night club is where Black Axe truly began, which is why you will see the word Bakken appear here and there. This is the rub for the Bakken Special (page 148), the Lamb Offal Flatbread (page 160) and the Adana Skewer (page 142), but it can be used for any type of slow roasted pork, poultry, beef or lamb.

ESSENTIAL EQUIPMENT

spice grinder or mini food processor

MAKES 50 G (2 OZ/½ CUP)

4 tablespoons cumin seeds
4 tablespoons fennel seeds
2 tablespoons coriander seeds
2 tablespoons caraway seeds
2 tablespoons black peppercorns
4 star anise

Toast the seeds in a dry frying pan (skillet) over a medium heat until they start to snap, crackle and pop and smell fantastic. Allow to cool.

Blitz in a spice grinder or mini food processor to a fine(ish) powder, then store in an airtight container. It will stay fresh for 1 week.

MISSION SPICE

This recipe has been slightly adapted from Danny Bowien's original recipe in *The Mission Chinese Cookbook*, mainly because I had to tweak a few things due to the availability of certain ingredients in the UK. Notably, the only red Szechuan peppercorns I could get my hands on absolutely suck. They lack any of the fragrance and numbing qualities that Szechuan pepper should possess, which Harold McGee describes as a sensation akin to 'touching the terminals of a 9-volt battery with your tongue'. They marry well with chilli and together produce what is know as *ma la*, which literally translates to numbing and spicy.

The US government banned the importation of Szechuan peppercorns between 1968–2005 because they are capable of carrying Citrus Canker. The ban was lifted in 2005, as long as they were heated to kill any bacteria. However, this treatment killed any flavour, and distributors haven't stopped pasteurizing them.

The green Szechuan peppercorns I have managed to find have a superior numbing property and fragrance. It's that numbing and spicy combination that I love, and judging by the rate at which our Buttermilk Fried Chicken Wings (page 123) are consumed, so do many of our customers.

ESSENTIAL EQUIPMENT

spice grinder or mini food processor

MAKES 200 G (7 OZ/1 CUP)

2 tablespoons cumin seeds
2 tablespoons fennel seeds
2–4 star anise
2 tablespoons cardamom pods
2 teaspoons cloves
4 tablespoons whole green Szechuan peppercorns
3 tablespoons caster (superfine) sugar
4 tablespoons chicken stock powder (bouillon)
2 tablespoons cayenne powder

Toast all the spices apart from the peppercorns in a dry frying pan (skillet) over a low–medium heat for 2–3 minutes, until they've coloured slightly and started to pop and become fragrant. Remove from the heat and allow to cool.

Toast the peppercorns in a frying pan until fragrant, then tip into a spice grinder and blitz to a rough powder. Sieve to remove the husks.

Mix all the ingredients together and blitz to as fine a powder as you can. Store in an airtight container. This mix will lose much of its potency after a week or so. Aside from the recipes here that call for it, this works well on any kind of eggs or mushrooms on toast, and as a rub for chicken, pork, or beef. I also sprinkle it over ready salted crisps.

AÏOLI

MAKES 300 ML (10 FL OZ/1¼ CUPS)

1 large egg
4 cloves garlic, chopped
250 ml (8 fl oz/generous 1 cup) sunflower oil
¼ teaspoon salt
juice 1 lemon, to taste

Crack the egg into a small bowl or the cup attachment of a hand-held (immersion) blender with the garlic and blitz on a high speed or whisk until incorporated. Reduce the speed a little and add the oil a drizzle at a time, until emulsified. Add the salt and the lemon juice, to taste.

Chill in an airtight container until needed; it will keep for up to 5 days.

LEMON OIL

MAKES 500 ML (17 FL OZ/GENEROUS 2 CUPS)

100 ml (3½ fl oz/scant ½ cup) lemon juice
400 ml (14 fl oz/1⅔ cups) good quality light olive oil

Mix the juice and oil together in a bottle. Shake well before applying. This will work as a light, stand-alone dressing in addition to lubricating dishes. Store in the refrigerator for up to 1 week.

TAHINI SAUCE

ESSENTIAL EQUIPMENT

hand-held (immersion) blender

MAKES 300 ML (10½ FL OZ/1¼ CUPS)

200 ml (7 fl oz/scant 1 cup) sunflower or vegetable oil
10 cloves garlic, chopped
100 g (3½ oz/¾ cup) tahini
lemon juice, to taste
salt

In a small saucepan over a very low heat, barely simmer the oil with the garlic and a pinch of salt, to lightly confit, until the garlic becomes nut brown, around 30 minutes. Drain the garlic and blitz to a paste in a small bowl or in the cup attachment of a hand-held (immersion) blender. Blitz in 100 ml (3½ fl oz/scant ½ cup) water then incorporate the tahini. Season with salt and lemon to taste. This can be stored in the refrigerator for 5 days.

ANCHOVY DRESSING

ESSENTIAL EQUIPMENT

hand-held (immersion) blender

MAKES 120 ML (4¼ FL OZ/½ CUP)

1 clove garlic
1 x 50 g (2 oz) can of the best quality anchovies you can find, chilled
1½ tablespoons rapeseed oil
juice of ½ lemon, plus extra to taste

Grate the garlic into a small bowl or the cup attachment of your hand-held (immersion) blender. Add the chilled anchovies with a little of the oil from the can and blitz until smooth. Emulsify the oil into the anchovies in one gentle, constant, steady stream. If you add it too fast you run the risk of splitting the dressing. Add 2 tablespoons water and the lemon juice and whizz once more on a lower setting just to incorporate. Taste again. Feel free to give it another squeeze of lemon if you like it zesty. When you're happy with the acidity, decant into an airtight container or squeeze bottle and chill until needed. It will keep for up to 5 days.

HORSERADISH CREAM

This can be made a day in advance. The fumes given off when grating fresh horseradish are going to make your eyes water a bit so get the crème fraiche into a bowl ready and waiting, once the horseradish is mixed into the crème fraiche the fumes will disperse.

SERVES 4-5

½ root fresh horseradish, grated
3 tablespoons crème fraiche
lemon juice, to taste
salt

In a small bowl, mix the horseradish and crème fraîche, then add lemon juice, a little at a time, checking the taste each time; it should be sharp, but not so zesty that it clashes with the heat of the horseradish. Add a little salt, then store in an airtight container in the refrigerator. It will keep for 3–4 days before losing its potency.

APPLE AND CHILLI SAUCE

This is the sauce we serve with the Crispy Fuckin' Rabbit (page 92) but it's magical with pork or pressed pig's head.

ESSENTIAL EQUIPMENT

blowtorch
mini food processor

MAKES 1 LITRE (34 FL OZ/4¼ CUPS)

300 g/11 oz medium-heat red chillies
4 plump cloves garlic
2 banana shallots
vegetable oil, for frying
175 ml (6 fl oz/¾ cup) cloudy apple juice
125 ml (4¼ fl oz/½ cup) apple cider vinegar
125 g (4¼ oz/generous 1 cup) palm sugar
3 Pink Lady apples, peeled and cut into 1 cm (½ inch) dice
soy sauce, to taste

Blacken the chillies with a blow torch, on a barbecue or under the grill (broiler).

Blitz the garlic and shallots to a paste in a small food processor. Add to a large frying pan (skillet) with a good glug of oil and cook until fragrant, avoiding any colour.

Purée the chilli and add to the garlic and shallot mix. Cook over a medium–low heat for 5 minutes, stirring occasionally, making sure the mix isn't catching.

Add the apple juice and cider vinegar and dissolve the palm sugar into the sauce. Simmer the sauce over a low-medium heat for 10–15 minutes, again being vigilant to make sure the sauce doesn't catch on the pan.

Stir in the apples when cool and add soy to taste. I add about 1 tablespoon of dark soy but find the salt levels vary from brand to brand, so add a little, then add more until you've achieved the level of seasoning you're happy with.

Pour into an airtight container and store in the refrigerator until needed. This will keep well for a week or so.

SWEET SZECHUAN VINAIGRETTE

I will go into work after being off for a couple of days, and Trick will have developed a better method to cook something, refined a sauce, or experimented with something new. It's the most fulfilling facet of the cooking process for me – experimenting. I came in one day to find something labelled 'Sweet Szechuan Vinaigrette'. I squirted some on the back of my hand, tasted it and was immediately hooked. I eat this on its own over plain rice, it's that good – particularly good on the leftover rice that's caught slightly at the end of service, when you realize you haven't eaten all day and you're absolutely famished. I love the way this works with octopus (page 94), but it is extremely versatile. Think cold roast chicken, pork terrines, duck, ham – anything that benefits from a little zip.

ESSENTIAL EQUIPMENT

old frying pan (skillet)
fine sieve

MAKES 300 ML (10 FL OZ/1¼ CUPS)

50 g (2 oz) green Szechuan peppercorns
250 ml (8 fl oz/generous 1 cup) rapeseed or sunflower oil
100 g (3 ½ oz/½ cup) palm sugar
1 tablespoon spicy Chinese hot chilli bean paste (also known as spicy broad bean paste)
100 ml (3½ fl oz/scant ½ cup) red wine vinegar
1 tablespoon Szechuan peppercorn oil (prickly oil)

In a heavy-based pan large enough to hold all the ingredients, toast the peppercorns over a medium heat. I like to take a slower approach when toasting Szechuan peppercorns, as the oil they release can burn and end up tasting bitter. Look for a touch of colour. You will be able to smell when the peppercorns are ready by the intoxicating aroma. If I could bottle that smell, I would smother myself in it like a teenage boy applies Lynx deodorant. Turn the heat down and add the oil to the peppercorns. This might bubble up and spit, so stand back, then turn off the heat.

In a separate pan (one you care a little less about) start a dry caramel with the palm sugar over a medium heat. When the sugar starts to bubble, after about 2 minutes, reduce the heat and cook for 1–2 minutes until caramelized – slightly too much colour and the vinaigrette will taste burnt. Remove from the heat and whisk in the bean paste and vinegar, dissolving all the sugar. Add this mix to the infused oil and allow to cool completely.

Pass the vinaigrette through a fine sieve into a squeeze bottle or jug (pitcher) and add in the Szechuan peppercorn oil. Give it a shake, then chill in the refrigerator until need. This will last indefinitely.

XO SAUCE

According to rumour, XO first appeared in Hong Kong in the 1980s. That's a fucking cool fact, because that makes it a relative newcomer to the vast and diverse cuisine of China. The term 'XO' is used to give Cognac a reassuring, exclusive edge and guarantee of quality. The same rationale has been adopted for the sauce, which can contain a multitude of expensive ingredients. It nearly always involves scallops and/or prawns (shrimp), but I've eaten sauce that contains tiny baby squid, anchovies, bacon, jamón and fish eggs, to name but a few. I am attracted to the lack of discipline and open interpretation of ingredients, and conflicted over what and who makes the best XO sauce. The result is that you'll rarely find any two XO sauces the same. The recipe below is obviously the best, although it's really more of a relish than a sauce. It's a bastardized version of the XO sauce I first made at Joel Wootten and Joel Humphrey's pop-up, By Way of Chinatown. Ideally it should be made a day in advance to give it a chance to mature. One of my favourite ways to eat it is dolloped on some leftover rice, but it goes well with all manner of pork, poultry and seafood dishes.

ESSENTIAL EQUIPMENT

hand-held (immersion) blender

MAKES 500 ML (17 FL OZ/GENEROUS 2 CUPS)

50 g (2 oz) dried baby shrimp (Jefi Gold brand)
50 g (2 oz) dried scallops
1 teaspoon fermented shrimp paste
250 ml (8 fl oz/1 cup) Shaoxing rice wine
100 ml (3½ fl oz/scant ½ cup) rapeseed oil
8 cloves garlic, thinly sliced
250 g (9 oz) red chillies, deseeded and finely chopped
2 tablespoons palm sugar
1½ tablespoons soy sauce
fish sauce, to taste
4 banana shallots, thinly sliced

In a small bowl, rehydrate the shrimp, scallops and the shrimp paste overnight (or for at least 6 hours) in the rice wine. Chill in the refrigerator until required.

Warm the oil in a medium saucepan over a medium heat then fry the garlic, stirring to prevent clumping and sticking to the base of the pan, until it starts to colour slightly and add the chillies. Continue to fry for 5 minutes.

While that's cooking, pulse the scallops, shrimp, shrimp paste and wine with a hand-held (immersion) blender or food processor. Stir into the garlic and chilli.

Simmer for 10 minutes then add the palm sugar and soy. Finish with a few dashes of fish sauce to taste. This is where you can balance sweet with savoury. I like a decent hit of fish sauce so tend to be generous with it. Remember, you can always add but it's hard to remedy if you're too heavy handed. The same with the sugar, if you like it a little sweeter add a little at a time until it tastes how you like it.

Remove from the heat then stir in the thinly sliced shallots. I like to keep the sauce vibrant so you'll notice we don't cook ours down too much like some conventional XOs available. This will keep in an airtight container in the refrigerator for 3 days.

FERMENTED BLACK BEANS WITH GINGER

This 'sauce', if you can call it that, goes well with fish, game, beef, pork chops, chicken and quail, and basically anything involving rice... a versatile condiment indeed.

MAKES 400 G/14 OZ

250 g (9 oz) fermented black beans
5 plump cloves garlic, thinly sliced
50 g (2 oz) peeled ginger, grated
2 red chillies, thinly sliced
50 ml (2 oz/½ cup) rapeseed or sunflower oil
50 g (1¾ oz/⅓ cup) palm sugar
2–3 spring onions (scallions), thinly sliced

First soak the black beans in 250 ml (8 fl oz/1 cup) warm water till plumped up and hydrated. This will remove some of the salinity and improve the texture.

While the beans are soaking, gently fry the garlic, ginger and chilli in the oil until just cooked, 2–3 minutes, avoiding any colour. Dissolve the palm sugar into the mix.

Drain the beans and discard the water. Add the beans to the pan, stir well and remove from the heat. Allow to cool, then stir in the spring onions (scallions).

Store in an airtight container in the refrigerator – this will last for 2 weeks, but the spring onions will discolour after a day or two as the mix matures.

SHRIMP SAMBAL

ESSENTIAL EQUIPMENT

food processor

MAKES ABOUT 1 LITRE (34 FL OZ/4¼ CUPS)

500 ml (17 fl oz/2 cups) sunflower oil, for frying
5 banana shallots, thinly sliced
10–12 plump cloves garlic, thinly sliced
50 g/2 oz dried baby shrimp
50 g/2 oz dried baby anchovies
100 g/3½ oz fresh turmeric, unpeeled and grated
1 tablespoon dried chilli flakes
100 g (3½ oz/½ cup) palm sugar, grated
10 red chillies, blitzed to a paste in a food processor
2 tablespoons fish sauce, to taste

Place a very dry sieve over a dry metal bowl. Pour the oil into a frying pan (skillet) over a medium heat and shallow fry the shallots until golden, around 8 minutes. Remove every slither with a slotted spoon and drain in the waiting sieve. When the shallots have drained for a minute or two, transfer to a tray lined with paper towels to drain further. Repeat this process with the garlic. Fry the shrimps and anchovies separately in the same oil – these will cook relatively quickly so be vigilant. Remove and drain any excess oil on kitchen paper. You should have a pile of golden fried ingredients on the tray.

Carefully drain the pan of oil through the empty sieve into the metal bowl. Give the pan a wipe, removing any debris, and return to a low to medium heat. Add around 250 ml (8 fl oz/1 cup) of the oil to the pan and fry the turmeric for 3–4 minutes over a low–medium heat until softened. The turmeric will turn a deep amber colour. Add the dried chilli and palm sugar to the turmeric and cook gently over a low heat for 5 minutes. Add the blitzed chilli and 100 ml (3½ fl oz/scant ½ cup) water along with all the fried ingredients and simmer over a low heat for 5 minutes. Add the fish sauce to taste. Allow to cool before storing in the refrigerator. Mature in the refrigerator for 24 hours before using. This will last at least 4–5 days.

DILL PICKLES

ESSENTIAL EQUIPMENT

sterilized airtight container, such as a Kilner jar

MAKES 20

10 spiky cucumbers, halved
2 tablespoons fine sea salt
1.5 litres (50 fl oz/6¼ cups) white wine vinegar
750 g (1 lb 10 oz/3¾ cups) caster (superfine) sugar
1 tablespoon yellow mustard seeds
½ bunch dill

Toss the cucumbers in the salt and leave somewhere cool for about 30 minutes. We use salt to draw out some of the moisture and give a better snap to the pickles. Heat the vinegar, sugar and mustard seeds just enough to encourage the sugar to dissolve. When the pickling liquid is about body temperature, add the dill, then allow to cool completely. Wipe the salt from the cucumbers, drain away the liquid and transfer to a sterilized pickling vessel, such as a Kilner jar. Pour over the pickling vinegar. Mature in the refrigerator for a week, then eat. These will keep indefinitely.

PICKLED RED CABBAGE

ESSENTIAL EQUIPMENT

sterilized airtight container, such as a Kilner jar

MAKES 500G/1 LB

1 small red cabbage
1 teaspoon sea salt
500 ml (17 fl oz/2 cups) malt vinegar
2 bay leaves
125 g (4½ oz/⅔ cup) caster (superfine) sugar

Remove the outer leaves, then very finely slice the cabbage. Place the cabbage in a large sieve or colander over the sink and using your hands, gently mix through the salt. Leave for 45 minutes–1 hour.

While the cabbage is salting, simmer the vinegar with the bay. Add the sugar, let dissolve then add 250 ml (8 fl oz/ 1 cup) cold water. Remove from the heat, then allow to cool to lukewarm.

Place the cabbage in an airtight container or sterilized jar and pour over the

pickling liquid. Store in the refrigerator for at least 24 hours before use, but this is at its best after 3 days.

PICKLED RED ONIONS

MAKES 800 G (1¾ LB/3 CUPS)

1 tablespoon salt
4–6 red onions, thinly sliced
125 g (4¼ oz/½ cup) caster (superfine) sugar
250 ml (8 fl oz/1 cup) red wine vinegar

In a colander or sieve set over a sink, distribute the salt over the sliced onions and let sit for 10 minutes.

While the onions are salting, dissolve the sugar into the vinegar in a saucepan over a low heat. When the liquid has cooled, add the onions. Tip into an airtight container.

These can be used after a few hours, but will be better after a few days in the refrigerator.

TURMERIC PICKLED ONIONS

MAKES ABOUT 400 G (14 OZ/1½ cups)

2 medium white onions, thinly sliced
1 teaspoon salt
250 ml (8 fl oz/1 cup) white wine vinegar
125 g (4½ oz/1 g cup) caster (superfine) sugar
1 teaspoon ground turmeric
1 teaspoon yellow mustard seeds

Set a small sieve or colander over the sink, add the onions and toss with the salt.

While the onions are salting, bring the vinegar, sugar, turmeric and mustard seeds to the boil in a saucepan, stirring the liquid at first to dissolve the sugar. Once boiled, take off the heat and allow to cool.

When the liquid is cool, add the onions and tip into an airtight container. They will turn a vivid yellow colour after a day or two in the refrigerator, but can be used a couple of hours after making. They will keep for 1 week, chilled.

SAUERKRAUT

ESSENTIAL EQUIPMENT

sterilized airtight container, such as a Kilner jar
saucer or plate small enough to fit snugly inside
the container

MAKES 1 KG (2¼ LB)

1 kg (2¼ lb) shredded white cabbage
1 teaspoon juniper berries (optional)
1 teaspoon caraway seeds
1 teaspoon black peppercorns (optional)
1½ tablespoons salt

Put the cabbage, juniper, caraway and peppercorns (if using) into a large bowl and sprinkle over the salt. Mix with your hands for a minute, then leave for 10 minutes. I normally use the time to sterilize the container for the sauerkraut. You can do that by pouring boiling water into the airtight container or jar of your choice and allow to cool a bit before pouring out.

Give the cabbage a final toss and transfer the cabbage and any liquid into your container. Place a small saucer or plate on top and press the cabbage down to displace the brine. Cover and leave somewhere cool and out of direct sunlight for 24 hours. The next day, pop the lid off and press the plate down again. The brine should be covering the cabbage now. Re-cover with the lid and return it to where you are storing it. Lift the lid every now and again to 'burp' the cabbage. Refrigerate after 2 weeks. If you like it really funky ferment it for up to 4 weeks. This will keep indefinitely in the refrigerator.

PICKLED SHIMEJI MUSHROOMS

MAKES ABOUT 450 G/1 LB

60 g (2¼ oz/¼ cup) demerara sugar
125 ml (4¼ fl oz/½ cup) rice wine
or white wine vinegar
300 g/11 oz shimeji mushrooms, trimmed

In a small saucepan, dissolve the sugar into the vinegar over a low heat, then allow to cool.

Once cool, add the mushrooms to the pickling liquid. You can store these in an airtight container in the refrigerator for a couple of days, or eat within an hour or two.

PICKLED GREEN TOMATOES

I'm not the fresh tomato's biggest fan. My highest appreciation of the tomato is in sauce form on a pizza or mixed through pasta, and of course in a decent Bloody Mary. I pretty much love anything pickled... except celery. Green tomatoes slice better than ripe ones, and I find the texture lends itself well to this treatment.

ESSENTIAL EQUIPMENT

sterilized airtight container, such as a Kilner jar

MAKES ABOUT 1.2 KG/2½ LB

250 ml (8 fl oz/1 cup) white wine vinegar
125 g (4½ oz/⅔ cup) caster (superfine) sugar
1 teaspoon fennel seeds
8 medium-sized green tomatoes thinly sliced

In a small saucepan, warm the vinegar, sugar and fennel seeds over a low heat until the sugar has dissolved. Allow to cool.

Place the tomatoes in the pickling liquid in an airtight container or sterilized jar and refrigerate. The tomatoes will be good to eat the day after preparation, and even better after 3-4 days.

PICKLED MOOLI

Up there with my all-time favourite pickles, this is a good combination of vinegar flavour with a decent fermented edge. A polite warning though... this pickle omits a powerful fart-like aroma when you open the lid after a few days in the refrigerator. It always tickles me when the smell catches people unaware and they start looking around suspiciously for the culprit.

ESSENTIAL EQUIPMENT

mandoline with ribbon attachment or vegetable peeler

MAKES 150 G (5⅓ OZ/1 CUP)

300 ml (10 fl oz/1¼ cups) white wine vinegar
150 g (5 oz/¾ cup) caster (superfine) sugar
4–5 star anise
1 red chilli
1 mooli (daikon)
1 tablespoon salt

Simmer the vinegar, sugar and anise over a gentle heat. Allow to cool completely.

While the pickle liquid is cooling, prepare the mooli. Peel the mooli then top, tail and slice in half widthways so

it's easier to manage. If you have a ribbon attachment on a mandoline that's perfect for achieving the bootlace strands we serve at the restaurant. Watch your fingers and use the guard when pushing the mooli through the mandolin. If you don't have one of these, use a vegetable peeler.

Put the shaved mooli into a sieve and toss with the salt. Leave to sit for 10 minutes.

Add the mooli to the pickling liquid, then store in an airtight container in the refrigerator. This pickle only needs a few hours before it's good to eat, but will last a few weeks in the refrigerator.

PICKLED RED CHILLIES

These pickled chillies cut through fatty meat and add the welcome hit of spice I'm always craving. We use them a lot at BAM. Reserve the vinegar to use in a salad dressing after you've used all the actual chilli.

MAKES ABOUT 800 G/1¾ LB

250 g/9 oz red chillies
350 ml (12 fl oz/1½ cups) red wine vinegar
175 g (6 oz/¾ cup) caster (superfine) sugar

In a small bowl, whisk the sugar into the vinegar until it has dissolved.

Blister the chillies under a hot grill, over the coals of a barbecue or with a blow torch, then cut into 5mm (¼ inch) chunks. Combine the chillies and vinegar in an airtight container and store in the refrigerator.

GLOSSARY

RECIPE NOTES

EQUIPMENT

INDEX

GLOSSARY

BIBER SALCASI

A paste made from roasted red peppers and salt, this is commonly used in Turkish food in stews and marinades; you'll find it online or in supermarkets.

BLACK CHILLI FLAKES

Also known as Urfa chilli flakes, they are from Turkish Isot chillies, and are very dark red (almost black) in colour, hence the name. Stocked in a lot of online shops.

BLACK LIMES

These are sundried limes that are often used in Middle Eastern stews to impart a citrusy flavour. I mostly use them whole or sliced, but they can also be ground to a powder.

BONITO FLAKES

Also known as katsuobushi, this is dried and fermented tuna, commonly used in Japanese cooking.

CHINESE HOT CHILLI BEAN PASTE (SPICY BROAD BEAN PASTE)

A mix of chillies and fermented broad (fava) beans, this paste is from the Szechuan region of China, and used in soups, stews and braises, and is one of the predominant flavours in mapo dishes.

DRIED BABY ANCHOVIES

Similar to dried baby shrimp, these anchovies give a whack of salty flavour, and can also add a bit of texture to a dish when fried. Make sure you get the really tiny ones – I use Jeeny's or Jefi Gold Pack.

DRIED BABY SHRIMP

Sun-dried, these tiny prawns (shrimp) have a strong savoury flavour and are used in a lot of Chinese and South East Asian dishes, so they are easy to find in Asian supermarkets.

DRIED HIBISCUS FLOWERS

Hibiscus has a slightly sour, cranberry-ish flavour to it, and is mostly used in drinks and desserts in Mexican cuisine. You should be able to find these in bigger supermarkets, or failing that, online.

DRIED SCALLOPS

Yet more dried seafood. This is also known as conpoy. They are used in southern Chinese and Japanese cooking, and offer a little more gentle sweetness than a dried anchovy, for example.

FERMENTED CHILLI SAUCE

Also known as sambal oelek, fermented chilli sauce is super hot, salty and a little bit acidic. Often used in Indonesian cooking, you can eat this as a condiment, or stir through marinades and sauces to beef up the flavour.

FERMENTED SALTED BLACK BEANS

A Chinese ingredient, these are soy beans fermented in salt – consequently, you'll need to rinse them before using. You'll find them in most decent Asian supermarkets. I use Lao Gan Ma.

FERMENTED TURNIP JUICE

Salgam suyu, as it's known in Turkish, can easily be sourced in Turkish supermarkets or online. It's salty and a little bit spicy, so subsequently pretty refreshing – you'll often find people drinking a glass of it with an Adana kebab.

GRAPE MUST MUSTARD

This vibrant purple French mustard uses grape must to add an additional piquancy to wholegrain mustard.

GREEN SZECHUAN PEPPERCORNS

I've had a bit of a rant about Szechuan peppercorns on page 197, and why you should buy green instead of the more ubiquitous red, so it's best to refer to that, but in a nutshell, this is the originator of the numbing sensation and perfumed, zesty aroma in a lot of Szechuan dishes.

GUINDILLA PEPPERS

A pickled pepper from the Basque region, they are often eaten as tapas or pintxos, but also do a good job of cutting through rich meat dishes or adding a little bit of mild heat.

KOHLRABI, PEANUTS AND TOFU IN CHILLI OIL

This is made by a brand called Lao Gan Ma, and is a chilli sauce of sorts. It can be used as a condiment, or stirred into meat or vegetable braises.

LOVAGE

A herb that looks and tastes a little like celery leaves. This can be tricky to source, so flavour-wise, if you are struggling, use celery leaves or tarragon, or a mix of both. This will also grow like a weed in the garden.

PICKLED WALNUT VINEGAR

This is simply the vinegar out of a jar of pickled walnuts. You'll find these in delis or online.

PIG'S BLOOD

There are restrictions on butchers selling fresh pig's blood in the UK, so you will need to buy this frozen online. I use the Cabalen brand.

POMEGRANATE MOLASSES

A sweet-sour syrup made from pomegranate seeds, mostly used in Middle Eastern dishes. A good addition to salad dressings and marinades, but also just for general drizzling.

PRESERVED BLACK BEANS IN CHILLI OIL

Fermented soy beans in a spicy oil, there's not much more to say, other than they are great for adding a little savoury smack to soups, stews and even more robust salads. Look for the Lao Gan Ma brand.

PRESERVED LEMONS

Citrus in a salt brine; fairly ubiquitous now, you'll find this Middle Eastern pickle in most supermarkets, or online. It's also pretty easy to make your own – again, you'll find methods for this online.

PRICKLY OIL

A Szechuan peppercorn-infused oil, I use this to pep up the Mapo Tofu (page 76), but you could also use it in dressings, or toss it through noodles, if you want a bit of that famed numbing sensation.

SALTPETER

Also known as potassium nitrate, this is a chemical often used in processed meat products to intensify the pinkness. Taste-wise, it doesn't make any difference, so I leave this as optional.

SHAOXING RICE WINE

Fermented from rice, you'll find this cooking wine in pretty much every major supermarket. It adds a smoky depth to sauces.

SHRIMP PASTE

Used a lot in Thai cooking, this does a similar job to the dried baby shrimps, but works well stirred into sauces for extra flavour with no contrasting texture.

TURKISH PICKLED PEPPERS

You'll probably recognise these from your kebab or falafel wrap. Use whole or sliced for a bit of heat and acidity.

RECIPE NOTES

The techniques and methods outlined in this book often require a bit of common sense and trial and error, in particular using barbecues, smoking equipment and making bread. Care should be taken around open flames, especially if children are nearby.

There are many variables at play when grilling, smoking or baking, from temperature and ingredients to the equipment used, and the most important thing to remember is that even if something doesn't go quite right the first time, it's worth trying again. Have fun, enjoy the process of cooking and learn from each of your new attempts.

All **MILK** is whole (full-fat) milk, unless specified otherwise.

PEPPER is always freshly ground black pepper, unless specified otherwise, and salt should be a good quality sea salt.

HERBS are fresh, unless specified otherwise.

EGGS are assumed to be large (US extra large) and preferably organic and free-range.

When using the zest of **CITRUS FRUIT**, buy unwaxed or organic.

Individual **FRUITS** and **VEGETABLES**, such as onions and pears, are assumed to be medium sized, unless specified otherwise, and should be peeled and/or washed.

COOKING AND PREPARATION TIMES are for guidance only, as individual ovens vary. If using a convection (fan) oven, follow the manufacturer's instructuions concerning oven temperatures.

EXERCISE A HIGH LEVEL OF CAUTION when following recipes involving any potentially hazardous activity including the use of high temperatures, open flames and when deep frying. In particular, when deep frying, add food carefully to avoid splashing, wear long sleeves and never leave the pan unattended.

SOME RECIPES include raw or very lightly cooked eggs, meat or fish, and fermented products. These should be avoided by the elderly, infants, pregnant women, convalescents and anyone with an impaired immune system.

When **STERILIZING** jars for pickles, wash the jars in clean, hot water and rinse thoroughly. Heat the oven to 140˚C/275˚F fan/Gas Mark 1. Place the jars on a baking sheet and place in the oven to dry.

When **NO QUANTITY** is specified, for example of oils, salts, and herbs used for finishing dishes or for deep frying, quantities are discretionary and flexible.

All **SPOON AND CUP MEASUREMENTS** are level, unless otherwise stated. 1 teaspoon = 5 ml; 1 tablespoon = 15 ml. Australian standard tablespoons are 20 ml, so Australian readers are advised to use 3 teaspoons in place of 1 tablespoon when measuring small quantities.

CUP, METRIC AND IMPERIAL MEASUREMENTS are used in this book. Follow one set of measurements throughout, not a mixture, as they are not interchangeable.

EQUIPMENT

BARBECUE

You will find detailed information in the grilling section about this (page 42), but all of the recipes in the book will work on a simple kettle or drum barbecue. You don't need anything fancy.

CAST-IRON PAN

A well-seasoned, cast-iron frying pan is essential in any kitchen for decent heat retention and crisp frying. The investment is well worth it for its versatility, given that it can be used in the oven, too.

CHEF'S PRESENTATION RING

For presenting in a neat circle on the plate. It's also helpful for cooking a crumpet. If you want to improvise, you can cut the top and bottom from a small tin can, being extremely careful of the sharp edges.

CLOCHE

A cloche is a domed metal cover that can be used on a barbecue to cover a small surface area, but is also useful for covering things on the stove or in the oven (depending on the size and material), and for retaining heat after something has cooked. Not essential, but helpful if you have the storage space.

DEEP-FAT FRYER

Some of you may be comfortable with the idea of a pan of bubbling fat on the hob, but I for one am not. A deep-fat fryer takes the stress out of cooking in oil at a very high temperature, so I always suggest you use this method when required.

DIGITAL THERMOMETER

Invest in one of these and your life will be a million times less complicated when deep frying or checking the internal temperature of cooked meat. They are surprisingly cheap, too.

DOUGH SCRAPER

Whether metal or plastic, this is extremely helpful for portioning dough, cleaning down work surfaces and easing dough off of pizza peels.

ELECTRIC SMOKER

You will find info on this on page 50. Do some research online to find what's right for you. You can get ones for both indoor and outdoor use. At BAM we use a Cookshack smoker.

GASTRONORM

A large, deep stainless steel tray used in professional kitchens. You can pick one up quite cheaply online or from a catering supply shop, or just use the biggest roasting pan you have when this is called for in a recipe.

INTERLOCKING LOAF PANS

I mainly use these for compressing terrines; again, you can pick them up at a kitchen shop or online for very little money, and it will make this task much neater and easier.

PERFORATED BARBECUE FRYING PAN

I use this to cook the mussels on page 112, but it's also very helpful for cooking vegetables on the barbecue if you want a bit of smokiness but not necessarily a full chargrill.

PIZZA OVEN

If you're not looking for a permanent installation in the garden, I would recommend the Roccbox by Gozney for a small portable oven, but when I built my own, I used the following books for guidance: *The Bread Builders: Hearth Loaves and Masonry Ovens* by Daniel Wing and Alan Scott and *The Community Bake Oven: A Community Process for Building a Bread Oven* by Geeta Vaidyanathan and Karin Kliewer.

PIZZA PEEL

A pizza peel or two will make your life a lot easier when working with sourdough with a high moisture content. You can pick one up very cheaply on Amazon, so in this instance I highly recommend you don't try to improvise.

PIZZA STONE

A pizza stone is essential if you are cooking flatbreads in the oven, as they will retain an enormous amount of heat, which ensures a crisp base. You can find them made of cast iron and ceramic, too.

SHARP BONING KNIFE

Used to butcher meat, especially helpful for intricate cutting of flesh away from bones with its very thin, sharp tip.

SILICONE MOULDS

I have recommended specific sizes for making the Peanut and Foie Gras Bar on page 176; a silicone mould is without doubt the easiest way to go for shaping ice creams.

TONGS

A stainless steel pair is essential for flipping on the barbecue; make sure you buy something with a decent handle.

TURKISH KEBAB SKEWERS

These skewers are wider and flatter than the usual ones. If you're intending on making the Adana Skewer on page 142, you will absolutely need to invest in these to ensure there is enough skewer surface-area for the loose mixture to cling to, or else the meat will end up all over the grill.

WOOD

At BAM, we use the London Log Company. When I first started smoking I would just use wood from my garden or nick it from parks and dry it out, but that's probably not good advice. You can source your own wood for smoking easily online. There is more information about wood selection on page 47.

INDEX

Page numbers in *italic* refer to illustrations

steamed buns
 smoked eel and horseradish squid ink
 steamed buns 118–19, *120*
stone, pizza 206
sumac shallots 197
Super Lyan X BAM Whiskey Sourz 189, *192*
sweet 168–81
 after dinner mint ice cream 172, *174*
 deep-fried mince pie *180*, 181
 peanut and foie gras bar with c_ _t
 biscuits 176–8, *179*
 rhubarb and tequila granita 173, *175*
 whiskey and honey ice cream 173
sweet chestnut 47
sweet Szechuan vinaigrette 199
sweetcorn
 charred sweetcorn and smoked cod's
 roe butter 108, *109*
Szechuan vinaigrette, sweet 199
 pressed octopus and Szechuan
 vinaigrette 94, *95*

T

tahini sauce 198
tartare
 beef tartare royale 138, *139*
Tas Firin 56
tequila
 Le Lagerita 188, *191*
 rhubarb and tequila granita 173, *175*
Thailand 14
thermometer, digital 207
thyme twigs 47
Tiernan, Kate 17–18, 19, 21, 24, 28, 65,
 153
tofu
 mapo tofu, hash browns and fried eggs
 76, *77*
tomatoes
 brown butter poached salt cod, gem
 lettuce, XO sauce 115, *116–17*
 ezme salata 144–5, *147*
 pickled green tomatoes 201
tongs 207
Travers, Kitty 176
Turkish kebab skewers 207
turmeric
 Pickleback 189, *193*
 shrimp sambal 200
 smoked eel and horseradish squid ink
 steamed buns 118–19, *120*
 turmeric grabbers 128, *129*
 turmeric pickled onions 200
twigs, harvesting and selecting for
 smoking 47

V

veal tongue
 BAM Reuben 72–3, *74–5*

Vietnamese scrambled eggs with sesame
 bread 68, *69*
vinaigrette
 sweet Szechuan vinaigrette 199
vodka
 borschtback 84

W

watermelon and pickled ginger 104, *105*
whiskey
 Pickleback 189, *193*
 Super Lyan X BAM Whiskey Sourz 189,
 192
 whiskey and honey ice cream 173
wood selection 47, 207
Woolley, Charlie 21
Woolway, Jonathan 114
Wootten, Joel 199

X

XO sauce 199
 brown butter poached salt cod, gem
 lettuce, XO sauce 115, *116–17*

Y

yogurt
 lamb offal flatbread 160–1, *162–3*

ACKNOWLEDGEMENTS

Dedicated to Kate, Kaswell, Nelson and Elvis.

A special thanks to the people without whom we would never have been able to open our restaurant.

Our parents Moira and Paddy Tiernan and Anne and Arthur Mullinger. There are no words...

Andrew Mullinger, Michael Mullinger, Katherine and Jennifer O'Neil. Pat Kelly and Adam Hazelton. Your DNA is engrained in the walls and fibre of BAM.

Tristram Bowden. BAM lifer. Bringing so much to the table everyday, the restaurant would not be where it is today without your contribution. Eternal thanks.

Florence Gardin. Above and beyond.

All the BAM fam past and present. Thank you for your daily input and continued commitment.
    Big up to Adam (the OG BAM chef), Maggie, Alec, James, Ben, Pav, George, Rav, Megs, Paxti, Euclesio, Theo, Kas, Mike, Katherine, Jen, Amanda, Rae, Florence, Mac, Will NG, Will, Ginger, Billy, Ed and Connie.

Our Families: Chunky, GT, the Thompsons, the Kellys, the Tiernans, the Burnses, the Hazeltons, Maggie and Brendan O'Neil, Jon Deal, the Harrises, Amanda Thompson, the Shaylors.

Our friends, lovers and exes (in no particular order, I just wanted to remember everyone that has been there and if I've forgotten you – believe me I will – I am absolutely mortified).
    Lisa Markwell, Charlie Woolley, Matt and Celeste, the Harrop-Glassners, Gordon, Tine and Falke, Paul Don Smith, Alex and Bobby, Mark Parr, Sam and the Hazelton design and build crew, Tom Gozney/Gozney Ovens, Zeren Wilson at Bitten & Written, Ed Smith at Rocket & Squash, The Skinny Bib aka Perm, Jon Spiteri, James Ferguson, Alethea, Tom Adams, Tim Siadatan, Lars Hinnerskov Eriksen, Jesper Storgaard, Nicolaj Grummesgaard, Ian 'legend' Moore, Michael Dahl, the Rotherhams, Fingal Ferguson and Gubbeen Farm family, Richard and the Harts, Fergus and Margot Henderson, Kitty, Trevor Gulliver, Ben Coombs, Magnus, Anja & Ozzy, Matty Matheson, Trisha Matheson, Reuben Dangoor, Danny Bowien, Brent Young, Ben Turley, Henrietta Lovell, Chris Grosso, Action Bronson, Meyhem, Alchemist, Ryan Chetiyawardana, Anette Moldvaer, Tratts and Coltman fam, Jordan Frieda, Billy Durney, Jason and Rae Lowe, Jonathan Woolway, Angela Hartnett, Neil Borthwick, Mam Sham gals Rhi rhi and Maria, the taste cadets Seapa, Keiran and Markus, Julian, Andrea Petrini, Ed and Zoe, Edwin Lewis, Big John, Jod, Kevin Kent, Oggi and J Lowe, Cappers and Weaver, Tom Pemberton, Kitty Travers, the Gillards, Trubs (for an evening I will never forget. xxx), all the crew from St. JOHN and St. JOHN B&W old and new, the Franks, Angela D. John and Diz, Kim and her Maison crew, Liane Plant, the Quo Vadis crew, the Golden Heart crew, the Rochelle Canteen crew, the Meat Hook crew, the Mission Chinese crew NYC/SF, Joe Beef and the Liverpool House and Vin Papillon and Maison Publique crew, the Nightmarket crew, the Burnt Ends crew, the Le Grand Bain crew, the Ten Bells crew, the Som Saa massive, the Smoking Goat massive, the Legs Crew rip, Fatty Cue crew rip, Mandy and the Sambal Shiok crew, Zak Pelaccio, Jori Jayne Emde and the Fish & Game crew, the Bubble Dogs massive, Salon crew, Acock Jones massive, Jed Smith and the Donna's crew, Claudia Cornali-Motta, Peter Pilotto and Christopher de Vos, and Clerkenwell Boy.

Big ups to everyone who has a positive input into this industry.

I'd like to thank all our customers and regulars for your continued support. Without you there would be no BAM.

I wrote the majority of this book on an iPhone 6 watching 'People Just Do Nothing', 'Ugly Delicious' and Anthony Bourdain's 'Parts Unknown'.

ABOUT THE AUTHOR

Lee Tiernan worked at London's iconic St. JOHN restaurant for 10 years, leaving as head chef of St. JOHN Bread and Wine in 2013, after deciding to pursue his own vision. He started with a Black Axe Mangal pop up in Copenhagen before securing a permanent site for his restaurant in North London, which has received critical acclaim and garnered an international fan base. Past collaborations include Momofuku Shoto Toronto, Joe Beef, Dan Barber's wastED, Action Bronson, Quo Vadis, St. JOHN and Mission Chinese Food.

Phaidon Press Limited
Regent's Wharf
All Saints Street
London N1 9PA

Phaidon Press Inc.
65 Bleecker Street
New York, NY 10012

phaidon.com

First published 2019
© 2019 Phaidon Press Limited

ISBN 978 0 7148 7931 4

COMMISSIONING EDITOR
Eve Marleau

PROJECT EDITOR
Lucy Kingett

PRODUCTION CONTROLLER
Sarah Kramer

PHOTOGRAPHY
Jason Lowe

DESIGN
João Mota

LAYOUT
Albino Tavares

Original artwork by
Reuben Dangoor (page 155)

The publisher would like to thank
Jane Bamforth, Emma Barton,
Vanessa Bird, Kate Calder, Sophie
Hodgkin, Eve Marleau, Emily Paul,
Tracey Smith and Hans Stofregen.

Printed in Italy

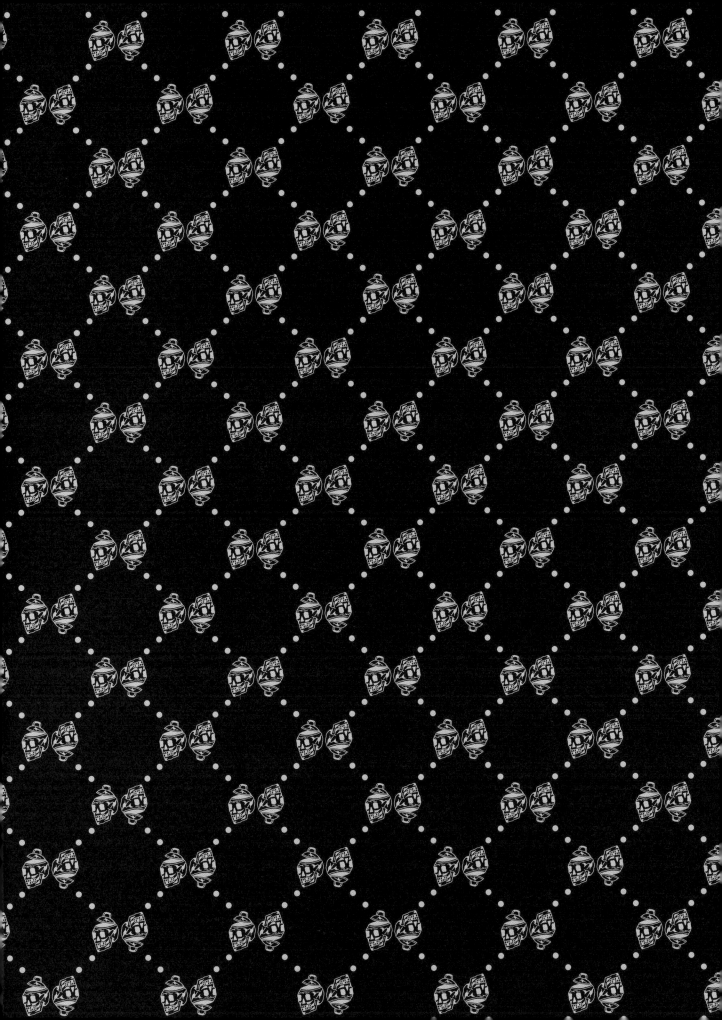

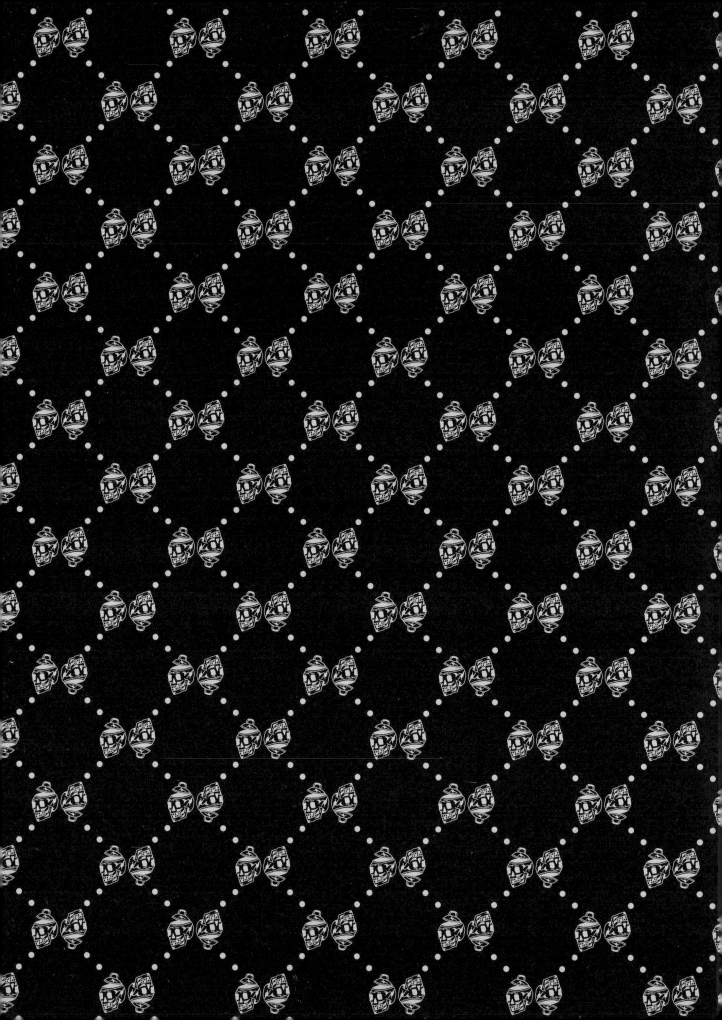